THE PUBLIC LIBRARY DIRECTOR'S HR TOOLKIT

ALA Editions purchases fund advocacy, awareness, and accreditation programs for library professionals worldwide.

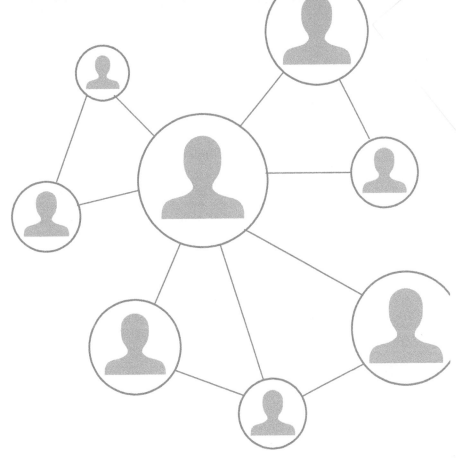

THE
PUBLIC LIBRARY
DIRECTOR'S
HR TOOLKIT

KATE HALL + KATHY PARKER

ALA Editions

CHICAGO | 2022

KATE HALL is the executive director of the Northbrook Public Library (IL) after serving as director at the New Lenox Public Library (IL) and in various library positions in the Chicagoland area for over twenty years. In her eleven years as a library director, Kate has been in leadership positions in state and national library groups including the American Library Association, Illinois Library Association, and Reaching Across Illinois Library System. She has served on the committee and chaired Director's University, an intensive training for new Illinois Public Library directors. Kate is the recipient of the 2021 Illinois Library Association Librarian of the Year Award and has just launched Illinois Libraries Present, a new statewide joint programming cooperative. She is the co-author of *The Public Library Director's Toolkit*, published by ALA Editions, and the devoted servant of one demanding cat.

KATHY PARKER was the director of the Glenwood-Lynwood (IL) Public Library District from 2002 to 2018 after serving as assistant director at the Harvey (IL) Public Library. She has worked in public and private libraries for over forty years in nearly every department and cofounded Director's University. She has served on numerous state committees including the Illinois Library Association and has served as library trustee for her local library and the regional library system, Reaching Across Illinois Library System. She was the 2016 recipient of the American Library Association's Trustee Citation award. After retiring in 2018, Kathy launched the kathyparker consulting firm, which provides training to trustees and new directors. She is the coauthor of *The Public Library Director's Toolkit*, published by ALA Editions.

© 2022 by Kate Hall and Kathy Parker

Extensive effort has gone into ensuring the reliability of the information in this book; however, the publisher makes no warranty, express or implied, with respect to the material contained herein.

ISBN: 978-0-8389-3839-3 (paper)

Library of Congress Cataloging-in-Publication Data

Names: Hall, Kate, 1979- author. | Parker, Kathy, 1963- author.
Title: The public library director's HR toolkit / Kate Hall and Kathy Parker.
Description: Chicago : ALA Editions, 2022. | Includes bibliographical references and index. | Summary:
   "This book will take you through the life cycle of an employee, providing a framework to develop your HR skills"—Provided by publisher.
Identifiers: LCCN 2021062374 | ISBN 9780838938393 (paperback)
Subjects: LCSH: Library personnel management—United States—Handbook, manuals, etc. |
   Library directors—United States—Handbook, manuals, etc. | Public libraries—United States—Administration—Handbook, manuals, etc.
Classification: LCC Z682.2.U5 H35 2022 | DDC 023—dc23/eng/20220111
LC record available at https://lccn.loc.gov/2021062374

Cover design by Kim Hudgins.
Text design and composition by Alejandra Diaz in the Gotham and Laski Slab typefaces.

♾ This paper meets the requirements of ANSI/NISO Z39.48-1992 (Permanence of Paper).

PRINTED IN THE UNITED STATES OF AMERICA
26 25 24 23 22   5 4 3 2 1

THIS BOOK IS DEDICATED TO
ALL THE STAFF WE HAVE SUPERVISED.

To our former staff:
Thank you for your grace when we struggled and learned
from our mistakes.

To those we work with currently:
Thank you for your continued support and feedback in helping
us be better leaders.

May we continue to learn and grow in our skills.
—KATE AND KATHY

CONTENTS

ACKNOWLEDGMENTS

WE WOULD LIKE to thank everyone who made this book possible.

To the attorneys at the law firm of Ancel Glink (Chicago, IL) for reviewing the book to ensure we were providing the most accurate legal information.

To our subject matter experts who provided feedback through the lens of an HR professional: Laurie Prioletti and Susan Walsh. Thank you for helping us appear, if only for a moment, almost as knowledgeable as you are.

To our Equity, Diversity, and Inclusion consultant: Biz Lindsay Ryan. Your thoughtful comments and insight helped us eliminate some of our own unconscious bias in the writing of this book.

To our wonderful editor at ALA Editions, Jamie Santoro, who helped guide us through writing a book during a pandemic and answered our million questions.

To our beta readers—Kelly Durov, Lynn Hoffman, Tim Prendergast, and Summer Kosuge. Your insight and feedback was invaluable.

To our friends and family for putting up with us when we struggled to meet our self-imposed deadlines and became (maybe) a bit cantankerous. We are so fortunate to have you in our lives.

INTRODUCTION

MANY MANAGERS AND directors receive no formal training on the Human Resources (HR) aspects of their job. While some libraries have HR managers or departments, at many libraries, managers and directors must go it alone.

Going it alone does not mean handling HR without professional help. In the writing of this book, we had the assistance of labor law firm Ancel Glink, two HR professionals, and EDI consultant Biz Lindsay Ryan who reviewed it to ensure compliance with the law and HR best practices.

This book will take you through the life cycle of an employee, providing a framework to develop your HR skills. As a manager or director, you need to know what will get you in legal hot water, and also need to develop the skills necessary to successfully recruit and develop staff. If you are new to managing people, this will be a significant shift as you move away from task-oriented work to focusing on how you can help the people you manage to be successful. Many managers and directors don't want to focus on the more uncomfortable side of HR, discipline and termination, but to effectively lead, you need to know how to do that as well. Throughout the book, you will find tools and resources to help you develop your identity as a manager.

Equity, diversity, and inclusion (EDI) should be central to our work in the realm of HR, but is often overlooked. HR is about hiring and retaining strong employees that bring different perspectives to the library. By putting EDI work at the core of your HR practices, you are creating a stronger organization that will increase retention and productivity. We have shared how you can incorporate an EDI lens into your employee processes and acknowledge that this is an area that we all need to continue to learn and grow in.

The journey is long, but the view at the end is worth it.

RECRUIT AND ONBOARD: CHAPTERS 1-6

In the first part of the book, you will learn how to lay a strong foundation for employees with job descriptions before turning to how to hire and onboard new staff.

DEVELOP AND RETAIN: CHAPTERS 7–9

Once you hire staff, how do you help them grow and extend their life cycle with the organization? We will cover individual development and retention, the importance of continuing education, and how to engage staff and strengthen morale.

DEPART AND REASSESS: CHAPTERS 10–12

Despite all your best efforts, sometimes employees will leave the organization. Knowing all the laws and when to apply them is critical to help navigate difficult situations. Looking at the full organization to assess what your staffing needs are and put a plan in place for when key staff depart will allow your organization to thrive. Handling discipline and, if necessary, terminations is often the most difficult part of being a manager. We will give you a solid framework for tackling these issues and cover the offboarding process before you go back to the beginning to do it all over again.

APPLYING YOUR LEARNING

We have included sample scenarios with questions at the end of each chapter for you to better understand and think through how to apply the information provided in each chapter. In this section, find out how we answered the questions throughout chapters 1–12.

THE TOOLKIT

After you learn about the life cycle of an employee, our Toolkit provides you with the templates and tools you need to create structure around your HR practices. You can also find more samples to help you in your HR journey on our website at www.librarydirectorstoolkit.com.

    This book will not give you all the answers, but it will set you up on a path to HR success. We hope you will share your struggles and successes with us at info@librarydirectorstoolkit.com.

—KATE AND KATHY

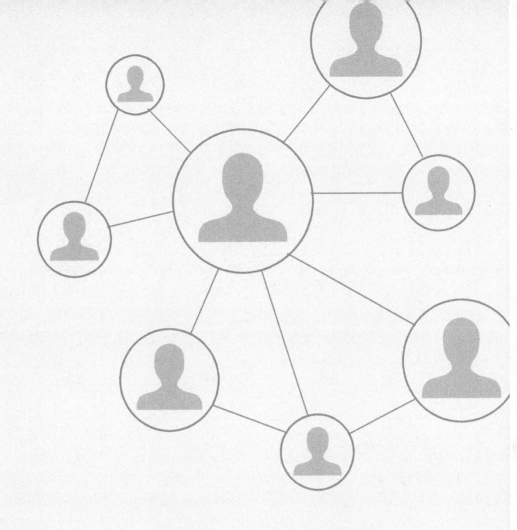

PART I
HR TOOLBOX
Recruit and Onboard

CHAPTER 1

Job Descriptions and Job Ads

After reading this chapter, you will know the following:

+ How to tell the difference between a job description and job ad
+ How to write an accurate job description
+ How to craft a compelling job ad

|||||||||||||||||||||||||||||||||||||||||||||||||||||||||||||||||||||||||||||||||||||||||||||||||||||||||||||||||||||||||||||||||||||||||||||

The life cycle of a library employee begins with a well-crafted job description and job ad. These set the framework for an employee's tenure at your organization. The job description will be used as a guide for the overall job responsibilities that the employee will perform and as a base for the salary structure of the position. The job ad is how an organization attracts talent. Effective job ads should contain information about the expectations and qualifications for the position, and include some information about the library and the community. The goal is to sell the position, library, and community to prospective applicants.

JOB DESCRIPTIONS

A good job description is the foundation for the position and outlines the essential functions. Every task and duty the employee performs is not listed; it highlights the areas where an employee spends the majority of their time. Position duties may change over time but the essential functions do not. A job description might say, "Performs collection management for assigned areas of the library's collection." A duty for an employee might say, "Collection management for board books and picture books."

ELEMENTS OF A JOB DESCRIPTION

The elements in each job description will differ based on the position (see figure 1.1). The description is written for the position, not for individuals who occupy the position. People will come and go, but job descriptions should reflect the needs of the organization, not the skills of a particular individual.

When crafting organization-wide job descriptions, check for consistency among similar jobs in the organization. When responsibilities mirror each other, use the same language. You also want to make sure that education and experience levels match for similar positions. Someone who works on programming in a children's department could have the same language in the job description as a programmer in the adult department: "Develops, produces, and evaluates programs to meet community needs." Review all of your job descriptions every few years to ensure that you are being consistent in your description of each essential function.

FROM THE DIRECTOR'S CORNER: KATHY'S STORY

The great library debate is the Degree vs. No Degree requirement. Each library will have its own philosophy. The requirement for a degree will be predicated on a few factors: community size, budget, past experience, and so on. I made the decision to make a degree for most positions *desired*, but not *required*, and sought work experience over a degree for most positions. This allowed me to be able to hire within the community, which is something I would have been unable to do had I mandated a degree for every librarian position. It also allowed me to stay within my smaller budget and hire more people, which in turn allowed my library to better serve the community. However, if the person hired showed aptitude for the work and a desire to go to school to get a degree, the library paid 50 percent of the tuition for the program. Focus on hiring good people for the organization regardless of degree. If an employee shows the aptitude and desire to pursue a library related degree, help them achieve it.

MORAL: Worry more about getting good people on staff first and less on whether they have a degree. Then help them get the degree desired.

FIGURE 1.1 | **Elements of a job description**

1. **Job Title**—What is the position title?

2. **FLSA (Fair Labor Standards Act) Status—Exempt or Non-Exempt**—An exempt employee receives an annual salary and is not eligible for overtime regardless of hours worked. A non-exempt employee is paid hourly or salaried, for actual hours worked and must receive overtime compensation for any hours worked in excess of 40 hours in a given workweek. A workweek is defined by the Department of Labor as Sunday-Saturday. Some states may have more generous overtime laws that you will need to follow. You should consult with an employment attorney when determining whether a particular position should be classified as exempt. Errors in properly classifying exemptions can result in costly wage and hour lawsuits.

3. **Union Status**—Employees should be told if the position is a union or non-union position.

4. **Reports To**—Who does this person report to as their supervisor or manager? This would be the person responsible for evaluating, providing feedback, and disciplining them.

5. **Requirements for All Employees**—Are there any requirements that all employees must comply with? Is everyone required to work one evening a week or be on a weekend rotation? What technology requirements do you have for staff? Do you have a staff code of behavior or values that staff must adhere to?

6. **Position Summary**—This is a one or two sentence statement of what the position does.

7. **Requirements for This Position**—What are the minimum requirements for a person to be successful in the position? A few examples are: general knowledge of library services; familiarity with online databases; having a working knowledge of a particular type of software (Word, Excel, etc.).

8. **Education/Experience**—What is the minimum education and experience for someone entering in this position? List if a degree or certification is necessary. When thinking about minimum education requirements, think through whether education is a requirement or an industry norm. Also consider the number of years of experience actually needed to do the job well. Is experience more important than education for the position or vice versa?

9. **Duties of This Position**—What are the essential functions of this position? Do not include all the duties, but do include the essential functions that anyone who occupies this position will be required to perform. These functions should be listed in order of time spent performing them. For example a youth manager will have "managing youth services staff" as the first item on the list as this is the function that they will spend the largest amount of time performing.

10. **Physical Requirements**—What are the specific physical requirements necessary to perform the essential duties of this position? When putting physical requirements together, think about the jobs through an accessibility lens and use language that is inclusive. Instead of stating, "must be able to stand for 4 hours at a time" instead try, "must be able to remain in a stationary position for 4 hours at a time." It is important to be clear about the physical requirements of a job as they often implicate considerations under the Americans with Disabilities Act (ADA).

WRITING JOB DESCRIPTIONS FOR AREAS OF INEXPERIENCE OR KNOWLEDGE

Writing a job description for a position you have little or no experience or knowledge in can be difficult. If you are creating a job description for an existing position, discuss the duties of the position with the person currently occupying that position and compile a list of duties performed. You can use this as a template for writing the description, but remember that job descriptions should be written for the position, not the employee in the position.

To write a job description for a newly created position, do research to see if anyone else has the same or similar position in a library or other type of organization. If you find a similar position, you may use the job description as a template for the newly created position. Make a list of essential functions, job duties, and experiences that you believe are desirable for the position. Some questions you can ask to help flesh out your description are:

- What will be the essential functions and job duties for this position?
- Is this position similar to any other positions in the library?
- Are there tasks that overlap with other positions?
- Is there a minimum education level needed for this position?
- Is relevant experience necessary or desired?
- Who will this person report to?
- Does this person have anyone who reports to them?
- Are they exempt or non-exempt?

WHAT TO AVOID IN A JOB DESCRIPTION

- Requiring a higher level of skill than is actually needed for the position
- Writing requirements based on the current employee who holds the position
- Listing every task performed
- Forgetting to list physical requirements
- Detailing how a certain task should be accomplished

An example of a good job description is included on our website at www.librarydirectorstoolkit.com.

JOB ADS

The job ad is what is used to attract prospective employees to your institution. A compelling ad should explain the open position including the basic duties and responsibilities, hours, salary, and basic benefits, in addition to including information about the library and community. Before writing the job ad, read over the job description and then make a list of skills and abilities your ideal candidate would have. This helps you further define what you are looking for in a candidate. For example, for a shelver position, you could list the following characteristics:

- High attention to detail
- Comfortable working alone for long periods of time
- Enjoys repetitive tasks
- Loves to put things in order

In the event that you have multiple positions open, consider whether you should mention why in the ad. Multiple openings could be a red flag to candidates. By explaining that the position is open due to a retirement, or that new positions are being added, you alert candidates that there are not a lot of open positions due to high turnover and a toxic environment. The goal is to attract the most qualified candidate for the position.

Often employers will create a job ad and use the job description as the ad. A job ad should always include a link to the job description, so that the prospective candidates can get a better feel for the job, but relying only on the job description does not give the library a chance to sell itself to potential applicants. A good ad should convey the pertinent details and give applicants a sense of the organization so they can determine if this would be a good organization to work for.

A good job ad should include:

1. **Position Title**—The title should be such that anyone can determine what type of job this is.
2. **Hours of Position**—full-/part-time, exempt/non-exempt
   List if the job is full-time and include if it is a 35-, 37.5-, or 40-hour work-week. If part-time, list how many hours per week. If a certain schedule is required, list the days and times.
3. **Basic Description of Duties**—Include the basic description of the job duties. It should not be an exhaustive list of duties, but just enough for candidates to get a good understanding of the duties for the position. A link to the full job description should be added so that candidates can delve further for additional information.

4. **Position Requirements**—Include the basic requirements to be eligible for the position: degree, experience, special skills, residency, and so forth. Give enough information for prospective candidates to determine if they are qualified to apply.

5. **Library Information**—Include details about the library including the type of work environment the library has (friendly staff, professional environment, etc.). What makes your library unique? In addition, listing your library's mission, vision, and values will ensure that applicants have a good sense of the library's culture. Then add some details about the community and links to community information.

6. **Salary**—Always include the annual or hourly rate of pay ranges for the position.

7. **Benefits Package**—List basic benefits for the position: vacation, sick days, personal days, pension, health care, and any other nonstandard benefits the position may have. Don't list the specifics of each benefit in the job ad. The specifics will be shared during the interview or job offer.

8. **Union**—Many libraries have union affiliations. Be sure to include if the position is part of a collective bargaining unit.

9. **How to Apply for the Position**—Be specific regarding what the requirements are for applying for the position. Does the applicant need to fill out an application? If they need to email a resume and references to a contact person, include that requirement and the contact information. This section is where you can put information on interview accommodations, which we will talk about in chapter 2 (Interview and Hiring Process).

WHAT TO AVOID IN A JOB AD

- Posting the job description as the job ad
- Listing every duty of the position in the ad
- Leaving out salary information
- Forgetting to include a link to the full job description
- Not linking to information about the community

A sample job ad is included on our website: www.librarydirectorstoolkit .com.

POSTING JOB ADS

Now that you have an updated job description and an enticing job ad, where do you post it so people can see and apply? At a minimum you should post the job ad on your library website and your social media platforms. Some other common places to post ads are:

- Local or regional library system
- State and national library association, including any specific caucus or special groups
- Local or regional newspapers
- Local job boards (chamber of commerce, workforce development programs, etc.)
- Online job search engines like Indeed, LinkedIn, and so on.

If your position is in a more specialized field that is not necessarily library related—such as a graphic designer, social worker, or IT professional—posting ads on platforms that are specific to those specialized fields can help. Investigate to see if there are associations for that field, newsletters, social media platforms, job search engines, and the like.

In order to gain a larger pool of diverse applicants, libraries must rethink where they are posting jobs. Getting a diverse applicant pool matters because more diverse companies perform better. According to a 2020 McKinsey and Company Report, "Companies with more than 30 percent women executives were more likely to outperform companies where this percentage ranged from 10 to 30."[1] Bringing more diverse employees into our libraries will benefit the libraries and communities they serve. Look beyond the usual job boards and seek out diverse job boards like wehere.space to get your job ads in front of as many eyes as possible.

Now that you have written your job descriptions and advertised your position opening, you are ready to gather the applicants and prepare for the next phase in the life cycle of an employee: interviewing and hiring.

HR LAW

The key law related to job descriptions and job ads that you need to know is the Fair Labor Standards Act.

FAIR LABOR STANDARDS ACT[2]

The FLSA establishes the minimum wage, overtime pay, and all employment standards for employees in public and nonpublic sector jobs. In order to determine if an employee is exempt (does not receive overtime), staff members must meet all of the requirements under the salary and duties test. Exempt employees should spend the majority of their time on managerial, non-repetitive duties. If an employee does not meet the salary test and at least one of the duties tests, they are considered non-exempt (eligible for overtime). For each of these exemptions, the employee does little routine work.

> **Salary test:** In order to be considered exempt, as of 2021, an employee must make more than $35,568 annually.
>
> **Duties test:** There are three tests for libraries to determine if an employee is considered exempt—executive, administrative, and learned professional.

1. Executive exemption—these employees must:
   - Be a manager or supervisor
   - Have their primary duty be managing a department or the entire organization
   - Customarily and regularly direct the work of at least two full-time employees or equivalent (FTE)
   - Have the ability to hire and fire employees
2. Administrative exemption—these employees must:
   - Perform office work directly related to the management or general business operations of the employer
   - Have decision-making authority on matters of significance
3. Learned professional exemption—these employees must:
   - Perform work requiring advanced knowledge (defined as work that is predominantly intellectual in character and that includes work requiring the consistent exercise of discretion and judgment)
   - Work in a field of science or learning
   - Have an advanced degree

The law always allows you to be more generous to an employee, and when it comes to exempt vs. non-exempt, the federal government considers making someone non-exempt more generous. When in doubt, leave the position non-exempt.

APPLYING YOUR LEARNING: JOB ADS MISSTEP

Beth was new to HR and posted a job ad for a computer lab attendant. She did not review the job description or ask the manager what they needed for the position before she posted the ad. It stated that the person needed to be friendly and have computer experience, but she neglected to link the job description to the ad. After several weeks she selected a handful of applicants to interview. She offered the position to Ben, a charming, friendly person who worked at his college computer lab and was able to start right away.

A few weeks into Ben's employment, the lab manager came to Beth and asked why she had hired him. He had been trained on the computer lab basics but did not have in-depth knowledge of computer programs like Excel or Word. In addition, he was not good with helping patrons with these programs and was often impatient and rude with the older people.

While Ben was very cheerful and had worked in a computer lab before, he hadn't worked with people who didn't know computer basics. Ben was just monitoring the lab and keeping supplies filled. He did not have much experience with instruction or how to use computer programs beyond his own needs. The manager asked Beth to terminate Ben and hire someone else.

QUESTIONS

1. What is the primary issue in this scenario?
2. Who are the players involved?
3. What went well in how this was handled?
4. What should have been handled differently? Why?
5. What laws might come into play on this topic?
6. How would you have approached handling this scenario?

KEY TAKEAWAYS

Job descriptions are the foundation of a position and should contain:

- Job title
- FLSA status
- Union status
- Reports to
- Requirements for all employees

- Position summary
- Requirements for this position
- Education/experience
- Duties of this position
- Physical requirements

When you are not familiar with the job you are writing a job description for or have a newly created position, research job descriptions for similar positions in other libraries or, if it's an existing position, have the employee make a list of essential tasks.

Job ads are focused on attracting talent and should contain:

- Position title
- Hours of position
- Summary of duties
- Position requirements including a link to the job description
- Library information
- Salary
- Benefits package
- Union
- How to apply

For both job ads and job descriptions, avoid being too vague and listing every task the employee needs to perform. When posting a job ad, consider posting in multiple locations to ensure more people see the ad.

REFLECTION QUESTIONS FOR CHAPTER 1

- Do I have job descriptions for each position in my organization?
- Do my job descriptions cover the essential duties of the position or all the duties?
- Have I included the appropriate physical requirements for the position?
- Does my job ad include enough information about the position, library, and community to attract qualified candidates?
- Where am I posting to attract qualified and diverse candidates?

ADDITIONAL RESOURCES

Gender Decoder for Job Ads. http://gender-decoder.katmatfield.com.

Kurter, Heidi Lynne. "Hiring Managers, Here Are 4 Useful Tips to Create More Inclusive Job Descriptions." *Forbes*, January 20, 2021. www.forbes.com/sites/heidilynnekurter/2021/01/20/hiring-managers-here-are-4-useful-tips-to-create-more-inclusive-job-descriptions/?sh=58bf49ed3586.

Maurer, Roy. "Crafting the Perfect Job Ad." SHRM, February 26, 2016. www.shrm.org/resourcesandtools/hr-topics/talent-acquisition/pages/crafting-perfect-job-ad.aspx.

Society for Human Resources Management. "How to Develop a Job Description." SHRM. www.shrm.org/resourcesandtools/tools-and-samples/how-to-guides/pages/developajobdescription.aspx.

Ward, Marguerite. "The Words and Phrases You Should Stop Using in Job Descriptions if You Want to Attract Applicants from Diverse Backgrounds." *Business Insider*, February 16, 2021. https://africa.businessinsider.com/careers/the-words-and-phrases-you-should-stop-using-in-job-descriptions-if-you-want-to/x3ee21m.

NOTES

1. Sundiatu Dixon-Fyle, Kevin Dolan, Vivian Hunt, and Sara Prince, *Diversity Wins: How Inclusion Matters* (McKinsey and Company, May 2020), www.mckinsey.com/featured-insights/diversity-and-inclusion/diversity-wins-how-inclusion-matters.

2. U.S. Wage and Hour Division, "Wages and the Fair Labor Standards Act Fact Sheet #17A: Exemption for Executive, Administrative, Professional, Computer & Outside Sales Employees Under the Fair Labor Standards Act (FLSA)," U.S. Department of Labor, www.dol.gov/sites/dolgov/files/WHD/legacy/files/fs17a_overview.pdf.

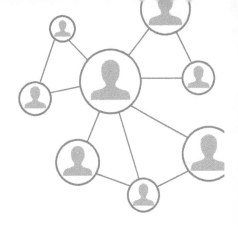

CHAPTER 2

Interview and Hiring Process

After reading this chapter you will know the following:

+ How to construct a hiring philosophy
+ How to prepare for interviews
+ What steps to take during the interview process
+ What happens after the interviews

||||||||||||||||||||||||||||||||||||||||||||||||||||||||||||||||||||||||||||||||||||||||||||||||||||||||||||||||||||||||||||||||||

Now that you've completed the job description and job ad, and have received the applications for the open position, you're ready to set up interviews, right? Not yet. There is more work to do before you get to meet the candidates. Ideally, this prep work should be done before the job ad is placed, but if you didn't do it then, complete it prior to starting interviews.

HIRING PHILOSOPHY

Strong employees who are aligned with the library's mission and values tend to be more invested and will stay longer. A hiring philosophy encompasses the values and goals of the organization as it relates to HR and will help with employee retention. The philosophy starts from the top and trickles down.

When considering your hiring philosophy, involve the managers and board to ensure it reflects the library's mission, vision, and values. Some questions to ask are:

• How do we value degreed professionals vs. people who have years of library experience and reflect the community being served, regardless of their educational experience?

- Will we accept professional degrees from other industries (teachers, business management, etc.)?
- How do we prioritize diversity in the workplace?
- Are we legally obligated to hire employees within our geographic district per a residency requirement?
- How do we prioritize supporting work-life balance for our employees?
- What salary and benefits do we offer?
- Do we value employee and departmental collaboration or independent work?
- How do we approach failure as an institution?
- How do we measure success for our employees?

Anyone responsible for hiring staff should know the organization's hiring philosophy when recruiting and interviewing candidates. This will ensure that the best efforts are made to hire employees whose values align with the organization. Occasionally, other factors may be considered when needing to fill a position quickly, creating a new position, or interviewing for a position that no one has experience with. If the people involved in the hiring process deviate from the library's hiring philosophy, someone may be hired who does not share the same organizational values, which can have long-term effects on the library, its employees, and the person hired.

FROM THE DIRECTOR'S CORNER: KATHY'S STORY

I was in the middle of a $6 million new facility project and found out I needed to have emergency surgery. My assistant director gave notice at the same time. I was feeling the pressure to get someone in before my surgery, and in an effort to move things along, I decided against doing a formal ad placement. I put out a few feelers about the open position and received a handful of applicants. I narrowed it down to two people: one was aligned with my management philosophy with little management experience, and the other candidate had management experience but a different management philosophy. I hired the person with more experi-ence and a different management style. I went into surgery thinking the library was in capable hands. When I came back after two months, the library felt off.

That "off" feeling never got better, and in fact it got worse. The staff were unhappy; I had made the wrong choice and eventually terminated the employee. My rash hiring decision negatively impacted nearly every aspect of the library, and it was my fault. When I interviewed candidates in the future, I made sure to involve staff in the hiring process and ensure that successful candidates were aligned with the library's mission, values, and philosophy.

MORAL: Hire slow and don't be afraid to own up to when you have made a mistake in hiring.

THE INTERVIEW PROCESS—BEFORE THE INTERVIEW

Now that you have several applicants for the open position, it's time to sort the applications and determine who you are going to interview. Employers have multiple software options to assist with their hiring. Keeping track of everything is onerous, and utilizing a good tool will help make an already stressful process easier to manage.

BEWARE OF UNCONSCIOUS BIAS

Everyone has unconscious biases. An unconscious bias, also known as implicit bias, is a social belief or stereotype of another person or group that is outside our conscious awareness. An example is thinking differently about someone of a particular race, socioeconomic background, or religion. In certain situations, employees may not be consciously aware of their actions or sentiments because they may not actively think about their surroundings. In these situations, employees may default to an unconscious bias that may not necessarily reflect their conscious values. Because it is unconscious, it is not always obvious to us.

When hiring, we need to be especially mindful of these biases and how they may affect our decisions. Sometimes managers can fall into the trap of hiring people who are very similar to them. This is called affinity bias. Our job as hiring managers is to create a process that removes bias. We want to bring in people who represent different backgrounds and ways of thinking.

Unconscious bias in hiring can be considered a form of unlawful discrimination. Employees involved in hiring must be aware of their actions to ensure compliance with local, state, and federal civil rights and antidiscrimination laws.

EVALUATION AND INTERVIEW RUBRICS

When determining who will be brought forth for interviews, you will screen the applicants based on the job description and who meets the qualifications and requirements for the position. Using a rubric based on the knowledge, skills, and abilities you are looking for in a candidate will help you reduce unconscious bias. Including a values alignment section in your rubric will allow you to evaluate applicants based on whether they share the library's values and philosophy of service.

When creating a rubric, start with the broad categories you need to assess and then break it down into specific knowledge, skills, and experience the candidates need to have. Table 2.1 is an example from the hiring process of a youth services manager.

You will also create a rubric for the interview itself. This one will be slightly different in that you will have scoring for each question instead of each category. However, since you will use the categories from the original rubric to craft the questions, you will be able to assess where people fall in different categories. While there are many different ways to craft an effective rubric, it can be challenging. The Society for Human Resource Management (SHRM)[1] has examples of hiring rubrics and a rubric creation worksheet is included in the Toolkit.

DETERMINING INTERVIEW NEEDS

You want to be cognizant of the time you, your managers, and the applicants spend on interviewing. Interviews are very important for both the employer and candidates, but you can overdo it. The interview process should not be a part-time job.

Interviewing should be long enough for you to gather the information needed to make an informed decision on the best candidate for the role and give the candidate an appropriate amount of time to assess what your organization is like and what the job entails. When planning the interview process, consider:

- The level of the position in the organizational hierarchy
- The number of hours the position requires (e.g., a full-time manager vs. a part-time shelver)
- What type of interview is best suited to this position (in person, phone, etc.)
- Who from the organization needs to be involved in the decision-making process

TABLE 2.1 | **Who to interview rubric**

CRITERIA FOR EVALUATING	SCORING	REASONING BEHIND SCORING
CRITERIA FOR SCORING: **Unknown/No Experience (1):** Did not indicate any experience/knowledge of key area. **Limited Experience (2):** Has some experience/shows familiarity with the key area. **Highly Experienced (3):** Has solid experience, mentions knowledge/skills/abilities that are at or above what is asked for in the job ad.		
MEETS MINIMUM QUALIFICATIONS 3 years management experience, worked with children, 5 years library experience	Yes No Maybe	
MANAGEMENT Mentoring and coaching Strong staff communication Handling challenging situations Leading with compassion	1 2 3	
YS SPECIFIC SKILLS Trends Kidlit knowledge Serving babies–seniors Professional development for oneself and others	1 2 3	
VALUES ALIGNMENT EDI Teamwork and collaboration Partnership building	1 2 3	
PROJECT MANAGEMENT Data-driven decision-making Delegating Project planning Prioritizing	1 2 3	
BRING IN FOR INTERVIEW	Yes No Maybe	

- What materials should be included for any special interviews (e.g., presentations for programming staff or design samples for graphics staff)

Whatever the process, tell the applicants so they know what to expect.

INTERVIEWING ACCOMMODATIONS

People with disabilities account for almost 20 percent of the population and are the largest minority group in the United States.[2] While legally people with disabilities can ask for an accommodation during a job interview, many don't for a multitude of reasons. Having more diversity on staff, including employees with disabilities, makes for a stronger organization. Taking steps to make interviews as accessible as possible will benefit candidates and help you hire a more diverse workforce:

- Put your commitment to accommodating candidates front and center in the job ad with clear instructions on how people can request an accommodation.
- When scheduling the interview, offer clear instructions and information on what will be asked of the candidates and what they can expect in the process.
- Consider where the interview is taking place. Is it accessible for people with mobility challenges?
- Provide the interview questions to the candidates to look over ahead of time.
- Consider an interview practice that provides an accommodation like a working interview where candidates try out the various job functions and get a tour of the space they would be working in.
- Make sure to only ask questions that relate to the skills needed to perform the job using "How would you do ABC?" questions instead of "Are you able to do ABC?" questions.
- Check your bias. What assumptions are you bringing to the table and how can you set them aside?

INTERVIEW QUESTIONS

When preparing interview questions, focus on the skills and abilities relevant to the position and design questions that will elicit responses based on a candidate's skills and experiences related to the position. As you craft your evaluation rubric, review each category and the skills and abilities needed and create questions based on the information you need to make an informed decision.

Interviewers should stay away from Yes/No questions. Provide hypothetical scenarios an applicant may encounter while working to evaluate their problem-solving skills and methods to accomplish tasks through behavior bases and skills assessment questions. Also, construct questions to determine whether the candidate shares key library values.

SKILLS-BASED QUESTIONS

- What tools and strategies do you use to stay organized in your day-to-day work and for projects?
- Describe what technology you use on a day-to-day basis in your work.
- Explain how you would change out a ballast in a light fixture.

BEHAVIOR-BASED QUESTIONS

- Describe how you would coach and mentor staff who are earlier in their careers and staff who are more established in their careers.
- If a patron requested the withdrawal of a book because of content they felt was inappropriate for children or for teens, how would you respond?
- Describe a time when you fostered teamwork and cross-collaboration in your work.
- Working on behalf of an organization sometimes requires you to enact new policies or take actions that you don't 100 percent agree with. Tell us about a time you disagreed with your supervisor and how you handled the situation.
- Describe a time when you had to work with someone who wasn't fulfilling their work duties and had to handle how it impacted your work.
- Give an example of a time when you failed and what you learned.

VALUES ALIGNMENT QUESTIONS

- Tell us about a time when you formed or strengthened a community partnership.
- Have you ever realized you had said or done something that may have been offensive to a colleague? How did you respond to that realization, and what was the outcome?
- Share a time when you gave feedback to a colleague or patron who was not accepting of others.

WHAT YOU CANNOT ASK

Title VII of the Civil Rights Act of 1964 and additional statutory updates to the Act[3] prohibit employers from discriminating against job applicants based on several protected classes. Asking a job applicant about their characteristics based on a protected class puts the organization at risk of committing unlawful discrimination. Employers should avoid questions relating to:

- Race
- Gender
- Age
- Religion
- Sexual orientation
- Gender identity
- Disability
- Country of origin
- Birthplace
- Marital status
- Family status (i.e.: Do you have kids?)
- Genetic information (i.e.: Do you have any pre-existing medical conditions or a history of diabetes in your family?)
- Pregnancy
- Previous workers' compensation cases

Certain states also provide additional protections. Employers should consult with their attorney to ensure compliance with federal and state civil rights laws.

Not only should employers avoid questions on an applicant's protected class, but they must also not discuss these topics if an applicant brings them up in an interview. Interviewers should strictly focus on a candidate's knowledge, skills, and abilities to perform the job.

Some questions you *cannot* ask are:

- Do you have any children?
- If you are working, who will pick your children up from school?
- What church do you attend?
- Will your disability allow you to perform these duties? (You can, however, ask, "Are you able to perform the essential functions with or without an accommodation?")
- When did you graduate high school?
- Do you own or rent your home?
- Have you ever had a workplace injury?

THE INTERVIEW PROCESS—AT THE INTERVIEW

Every interaction you have with a candidate is an opportunity to learn more about them and to sell the library to them. During the interview phase, candidates aren't the only ones getting looked over. They are also looking over the library's website, staff makeup, environment during the interview, and more to determine if it is a place they want to work. As mentioned earlier, selecting a person who aligns with the library's values and goals will make for a stronger organization.

INTERVIEWING: ROUND ONE

Minimally, one interview will take place to meet candidates. Be sure to let the applicant know what will happen during the interview, such as who will be involved and if you'll offer a library tour. It's a good idea to involve staff in the interview and solicit their feedback on the candidates. A good way to do this is to have someone give the candidate a tour of the library/department either before or after the interview. This gives the candidates a chance to learn more about the library and hear directly from staff about the library's culture and operations.

During the interview, the interviewer should:

- Provide a high-level overview of the library and the position including restating the salary
- Share what library-wide and department projects are or will be happening
- Go through the interview questions and ask follow-up questions where appropriate, based on their responses
- Offer the candidate a chance to ask questions
- Provide a timeline for the search and next steps and any other details about the position that the candidate should know

After interviewing the candidates, review your notes and scoring matrix to determine who should be chosen as the successful candidate. If there is only one round of interviews, skip ahead to reference checks or move to the next and final round of interviews. At this point there are usually two or three candidates.

INTERVIEWING: ROUND TWO

Not all positions will require a second interview. Typically, two interviews are reserved for higher-level staff, staff that work with multiple departments, or positions that require more technical skills. The second round of interviews is where a presentation would be done, or interviews with managers, departments, or staff (rarely) would happen. When involving staff in the interview process, only ask for their feedback if you are going to use it in the decision-making process. If asking candidates to prepare a short presentation or show a sample work product, be sure to tell them that it is not to be a lengthy presentation and should only take thirty to sixty minutes to complete.

THE INTERVIEW PROCESS—AFTER THE INTERVIEW

Once the interviews are complete, it's time to compare notes and select your new employee. Gather your notes and your manager(s) and work through each candidate and score accordingly. By using a scoring system based off your rubric, you are evaluating each person based on their experience, responses to each question, and merits. This helps prevent unconscious bias or discrimination in the decision-making process. As you progress through the scoring process, a lead candidate should emerge. You should also determine if a second choice exists in the event that the first candidate turns down the offer of employment.

REFERENCE/PAST EMPLOYER CHECKS

When you pick a candidate, ask the applicant for references. Because hiring processes often take months for some positions, do not ask for references until you are ready to call them.

Think about how much weight the checks will be given in the overall evaluation of the candidate. Know that sometimes what you don't hear when asking questions can sometimes tell you more than what you do hear.

When calling references, have a list of questions ready so that you can record the responses. You want to be respectful of their time and ask questions that are open-ended to elicit more responses and help you identify any issues. Some sample opening and closing questions to ask are:

- Can you verify the details of the candidate's employment (position, start and end dates)?
- When and where did you work with the candidate?
- What was your relationship with the candidate?
- Can you tell me what their duties were?
- Would you rehire them if given the opportunity?
- Do you have anything else you would like to add?

Be aware that some people may not be willing to answer some or all of your questions. There is always a fear of litigation if a reference or past employer gives negative information that may result in the candidate not being hired. As long as the information is truthful, this should be a minimal worry.

DON'T RUSH TO HIRE

Even with a thoughtful and thorough interview process, there are times when there are no viable candidates to offer the position to. If this happens, you can do a few things:

1. Review the applicants again and determine if there is anyone else you'd like to interview. Call them in for an interview and see what happens. Sometimes that overlooked candidate on paper really shines in person and could be a great choice.
2. Repost for the position and restart the search. Hopefully there has been enough of a lag between the first and second posting that more or different people will apply.
3. Rethink the position and what you are looking for. Is there something in the position or in your ideal applicant that can be adjusted that will attract other applicants?

It is better to take the extra time to reevaluate and repost than hire someone who won't be successful in the position.

MAKING THE OFFER

Now that a preferred candidate has been selected, determine an appropriate salary based on your salary schedule. This is also the time to put together the benefits package. We will discuss salaries and benefits in chapter 3. Contact that candidate and extend the offer to them, contingent on a background check. Explain the salary and benefits package. The candidate may try to negotiate the offer details so be sure to have determined the limits of your negotiation before you extend the offer.

Your preferred candidate has accepted your offer and you have set a start date. Now it is time to conduct a background check and, if your organization requires it, a drug panel. At this stage, make sure that your current policies reflect drug testing changes in state or federal law. As more states legalize or decriminalize cannabis possession and usage, basing a hiring decision on a candidate's cannabis consumption may violate state laws. Consult your attorney before making a decision based on a positive drug test.

WHAT IF THEY SAY NO?

Even after the best selection and interview process there are times when your ideal candidate turns you down. It may be because the salary or benefits package wasn't ideal for the candidate. It may be that they weren't feeling the same about the library as you were about them. They may have received a better offer.

Thank the first candidate for their response and then move on to contacting the second choice, reviewing the applicant pool again, or reposting.

There is a lot of preparation that goes into hiring new employees. The culmination of the process is the notification to the other applicants that a candidate has been chosen. The next area is to work on salaries and benefits—a critical part of attracting and retaining good employees.

Once the candidate accepts, notify the other applicants of the decision.

HR LAW

The key law related to interviewing that you need to know is the Equal Employment Opportunity Commission.

EQUAL EMPLOYMENT OPPORTUNITY COMMISSION

The Equal Employment Opportunity Commission is the federal agency responsible for enforcing the federal laws that prevent discrimination of an applicant or employee because of the person's race, color, religion, sex (including pregnancy, transgender status, and sexual orientation), national origin, age (forty or older), disability, or genetic information. Check your state's civil rights statutes as some states offer additional protections to certain classifications.

APPLYING YOUR LEARNING: HIRING FOR ALL ABILITIES

Due to a recent retirement in Technical Services, a new clerk was needed. The director, Lois, wanted to work with an employment organization that did job placements for people with disabilities, but the manager, Perry, was concerned that whoever was placed in the role would require too much support and other staff would end up having to do the work. Lois asked Perry to have an open mind and continue with the process.

The employment organization asked the library to accommodate Jimmy and do a working interview where the duties of the position would be demonstrated; then he had a chance to try out the task. Perry took Jimmy on a tour of the department, showed him where he would be working, and introduced him to other staff.

After the interview, Jimmy was excited about the job and Perry agreed that he had shown he could do the essential job functions. Perry offered the job to Jimmy and worked out that there would be a job coach with him the first two weeks. The job coach reached out ahead of time and worked with Perry to create training manuals to help with onboarding.

The onboarding was a success and soon Jimmy was performing the essential tasks more quickly and accurately than anyone previously in the position. But he was not happy. No one in the department talked to him and he sometimes heard people whispering and gesturing at him. After a couple of months, he gave his notice, citing that he did not feel comfortable working in the department.

QUESTIONS

1. What is the primary issue in this scenario?
2. Who are the players involved?
3. What went well in how this was handled?
4. What should have been handled differently? Why?
5. What laws might come into play on this topic?
6. How would you have approached handling this scenario?

KEY TAKEAWAYS

Before interviewing someone, ensure your library has crafted a hiring philosophy that reflects the library's mission, vision, and values and then prepare for the interview:

- Craft a list of knowledge, skills, and characteristics for the position.
- Create a rubric to remove unconscious bias when evaluating candidates.

- Write behavior-based and skills-assessment interview questions.
- Determine what the interview process is going to look like.
- Make sure you never ask interview questions about an applicant's protected class.

During the interview, use a scoring rubric to take notes. Following the interview, review your notes, check references, and then make an offer to your preferred candidate.

REFLECTION QUESTIONS FOR CHAPTER 2

- Does our organization have a hiring philosophy?
- Have I thought about any unconscious biases I have?
- How can we make our hiring process more accessible and inclusive?
- Have I created interview questions that are behavioral or skill based?

ADDITIONAL RESOURCES

Knight, Rebecca. "The Right Way to Check Someone's References." *Harvard Business Review*, July 29, 2016. https://hbr.org/2016/07/the-right-way-to -check-someones-references.

Society of Human Resources Management. "Template: Writing Behavioral Interview Questions." SHRM Educational Programs. www.shrm.org/Learning AndCareer/learning/Documents/Template_Behavioral%20Interview% 20Questions.pdf.

U.S. Equal Employment Opportunity. "Job Applicants and the ADA." www.eeoc.gov/ laws/guidance/job-applicants-and-ada.

NOTES

1. Society for Human Resource Management, "Template: Rating and Scoring Behavioral Interview Questions," SHRM Educational Programs, www.shrm.org/ LearningAndCareer/learning/Documents/Template_Ratings.pdf.
2. Office of Disability Employment Policy, "Diverse Perspectives: People with Disabilities Fulfilling Your Business Goals," U.S. Department of Labor, www .dol.gov/agencies/odep/publications/fact-sheets/diverse-perspectives -people-with-disabilities-fulfilling-your-business-goals.
3. U.S. Equal Employment Opportunity Commission, "3. Who Is Protected from Employment Discrimination?," www.eeoc.gov/employers/small-business/ 3-who-protected-employment-discrimination.

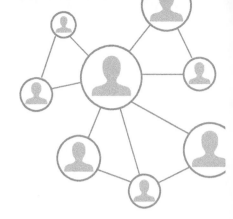

CHAPTER 3

Salary and Benefits

After reading this chapter you will know the following:

+ What a total compensation package is
+ How to place new hires in the salary schedule
+ What types of benefits you can offer
+ What the legal requirements about salary and benefits are

||||||||||||||||||||||||||||||||||||||||||||||||||||||||||||||||||||||||||||||||||||||||||||||||||||||||||||||||||||||||||||||||||||||||||||||||||||||||||||||||||||

When hiring a new employee, you need to consider what their pay will be and what types of benefits you will be able to offer. Together, salary and benefits make up the total compensation package. Many people only think of the salary when considering a job, but benefits can account for 20 to 30 percent of total compensation.

COMPENSATION PHILOSOPHY

In order to understand how salary and benefits intersect, you need to develop a compensation philosophy: a written philosophy that outlines how to treat employees regarding salaries and benefits. A compensation philosophy will help reinforce the library's values, aiding the library in attracting, retaining, and motivating employees.

When considering your compensation philosophy, involve the managers and board to ensure it reflects the library's aspirations and current reality:

- Regarding salaries, does the library want to be ahead of the market? Lagging? On target?
- What benefits can you offer employees to help with retention?

- Do you want to focus on a robust benefits package or higher salaries if you can't do both?
- What is the library able to afford in terms of salaries?
- How are you reflecting the library's values in the compensation package?
- Is the compensation package equitable?
- Does the compensation philosophy comply with all legal require-ments?
- How do you address increases and years of service?

COMPENSATION ASPIRATIONS VS. REALITY

Once a compensation philosophy has been created, the next step is to deter-mine what compensation and benefits the library can actually offer employees. The goal should be to offer competitive salaries with a great benefits package; the reality is that your library's financial situation will determine what you can afford. You might have very high benefits while salaries remain low or you might see salaries and benefits more evenly distributed.

Knowing the library's fiscal position will ensure you are not overpromising and under-delivering to staff. You may be able to offer a robust benefits pack-age but have to keep salaries lower. Once you have determined where you fall on the pay vs. benefits scale, you will set up your salary and benefits package.

SALARY

Before you can make a job offer to a prospective candidate, a salary must be determined based on the salary schedule. A salary schedule is a listing of salary ranges by position or grade and is the key to developing and maintaining fair and equitable pay for your organization. Each pay grade will have the job titles that match that range with a minimum, midpoint, and maximum. Those can be best described in the following way:

> **Minimum:** employees just starting in their field, who are still learning and may lack certain skills and experience
>
> **Midpoint:** competent performers who meet all of the requirements and perhaps a little more; this is where you should aim to have people paid if possible
>
> **Maximum:** top performers and those who have been with your library for a significant length of time

MINIMUM WAGE

Many states have passed graduated increases to the minimum wage. Make sure the correct minimum wage is reflected in the salary schedule. Be mindful of wage compression, which creates pay differences that are too small to be equitable among pay grades and can result in new employees making the same or more than staff with more experience.

In some instances, if the library is a department of municipal government, they may be required to follow the salary schedule of the larger organization. If your library has a labor union, the union contract will lay out terms regarding staff pay.

A salary schedule can be created through several different methods, but the industry standard is a salary benchmarking process. The method compares job descriptions to established salary surveys to identify the appropriate salary for a position.

Having a written salary schedule helps ensure that all employees are treated equitably when assigning salaries, and prevents administrators from making biased decisions based on previous salary histories or jobs. Many states now prohibit potential employers from asking about an employee's salary history and hopefully all will soon follow, ensuring that unequal pay does not carry forward from one job to the next.

FROM THE DIRECTOR'S CORNER—KATE'S STORY

When I started at one library, there was no salary schedule. The salaries were all over the place for the same positions. After creating job descriptions and doing a salary schedule with an HR consultant, we learned that 20 percent of the staff were above the maximum of the salary range, and 15 percent were below the minimum. Some of the staff below the minimum had been working at the library for a decade.

Because of the significant cost to correct the salaries, it took several years before we were able to get salaries in line with where they should be.

MORAL: Having a regularly updated salary schedule will prevent you from making biased pay decisions.

TABLE 3.1 | **Sample salary schedule, based on a thirty-five-hour workweek**

PAY GRADE	FLSA	JOB TITLE	RANGE MINIMUM	RANGE MIDPOINT	RANGE MAXIMUM
1	NE	Shelver	$19,984	$24,980	$29,976
			$10.98	$13.73	$16.47
2		Reserved for future restructuring	$22,480	$28,100	$33,720
			$12.35	$15.44	$18.53
3	NE	Clerk	$25,288	$31,610	$37,932
			$13.89	$17.37	$20.84
4		Reserved for future restructuring	$28,447	$35,558	$42,670
			$15.63	$19.54	$23.45
5	NE	Library Assistant	$32,000	$40,000	$48,000
	NE	Maintenance Worker	$17.58	$21.98	$26.37
6	NE	Administrative Assistant	$35,997	$44,996	$53,995
	NE	Maker Specialist	$19.78	$24.72	$29.67
7	NE	Graphic Designer	$40,493	$50,616	$60,739
			$22.25	$27.81	$33.37
8	NE	Librarian	$45,551	$56,938	$68,326
			$25.03	$31.28	$37.54
9		Reserved for future restructuring	$51,240	$64,050	$76,861
			$28.15	$35.19	$42.23
10	E	Circulation Manager	$57,641	$72,051	$86,461
	E	Human Resources Manager	$31.67	$39.59	$47.51
	E	Business Manager			
11	E	Department Manager	$64,840	$81,050	$97,260
			$35.63	$44.53	$53.44
12	E	Assistant Director	$72,939	$91,174	$109,409
			$40.08	$50.10	$60.11
13		Reserved for future restructuring	$82,050	$102,562	$123,075
			$45.08	$56.35	$67.62
14		Reserved for future restructuring	$92,298	$115,373	$138,447
			$50.71	$63.39	$76.07
15	E	Executive Director	$103,827	$129,784	$155,740
			$57.05	$71.31	$85.57

PREPARING A SALARY SCHEDULE

When creating a salary schedule through a compensation benchmarking process, you should ask who is going to do the study.

When determining who should do the study, the question must be asked, "How confident are we in the knowledge and expertise of this person(s) in this area?" The study should be in effect for three to five years, so make sure there is confidence in the process and methodology of whoever is doing the study. If hiring an outside consultant, the fees are usually based on the number of job descriptions being benchmarked.

Salary benchmarking projects are built using job descriptions. What is "benchmarked" is the data listed in the job descriptions, so if the descriptions are out of date or don't reflect the true duties of the position, the results will not be accurate. Without good job descriptions, the benchmarking could be compromised.

IMPLEMENTING THE NEW SALARY SCHEDULE

Once a salary schedule is created, it should go to the board for review and eventual approval. After the board reviews the new salary ranges, explain the new salary schedule to managers. Listen to the managers' feedback on the salary schedule. If they provide feedback that helps you realize that a position has been incorrectly assigned, change it. Have flexibility while staying within the set guidelines.

A difficult part of a project like this is deciding on a strategy for people that are at or above their maximum pay. There are a few options for handling these situations.

1. Freeze them at the top of the range. (This could also mean moving them down to the top of the range.)
2. Freeze them at the top of the range and pay a bonus based on the amount over the range. (This is generous to employees and not overly onerous to libraries.)
3. Let them continue getting a raise every year over and above the salary schedule with no cap. (Not advisable.)

After providing managers with the salary schedule and explaining how it will be implemented, share the salary schedule with staff. At this point, each staff member should receive written information on where they fall on the salary schedule and what, if any, adjustments or freezes will be made. Meet with each staff member who has had an adjustment or freeze and explain what that means for them. Ideally, management had previously informed the staff of the salary study project while underway.

USING THE SALARY SCHEDULE WITH NEW HIRES

When hiring a new employee, much will depend on the compensation philosophy discussed earlier; the education requirements of the position and the experience of the new hire will determine where they land within the salary range for their position. If they are just out of school with no library experience, they would be at the minimum for the position grade. If they have some experience, move them farther up the scale. You want to make sure you have internal pay equity, which means that if you are hiring a new person who has five years of experience in the field and you have an employee performing the same job that has been there for five years, their pay should be roughly equal. Again, if the library is a department of a larger municipal government or if staff are in a bargaining unit, the director may not have the flexibility to adjust the pay and may have mandates on what salary to offer.

NEGOTIATING SALARY

When offering a position to a job applicant, know ahead of time whether you are willing to negotiate on the salary. If the salary is non-negotiable, state that up front. If there is room for negotiation, make sure that if you go higher, you are creating an equitable environment within your organization.

If you are only able to bring someone in at the minimum, but have a little flexibility, be sure to know how high you are willing to go in the event they ask for more compensation. This is where your compensation philosophy comes in. If giving the applicant a significant bump would put them out of line with where existing staff with similar experience are, you need to consider whether that would create pay inequity in your organization.

Consider also that men tend to negotiate for salaries more than women[1] and ensure that your pay is fair with your first offer. Don't wait to have them ask for more money, but pay them what they should be paid based on their skills, knowledge, and experience. Thinking about this before you make the offer will ensure that you do not react in the moment and create a situation that leads to issues down the road.

USING THE SALARY SCHEDULE IN YOUR DAILY WORK

A salary compensation and benchmarking project usually has a shelf life of three to five years, with annual adjustments made for cost-of-living increases. However—and this is critical—you will need to regularly benchmark the compensation rates of key jobs, hard-to-fill jobs, and any position that may struggle to retain staff. These might include jobs in IT, graphic design, or makerspaces.

Any new positions added after the study will need to be benchmarked to determine the pay grade. An HR consulting firm will typically charge a flat rate for a single job description. Any HR consulting firm that does the study should also provide at least three years of updates to the salary schedule based upon market changes.

BENEFITS

Salary is the first half of a total compensation package, and benefits is the second. Benefits can vary widely by library, but they should be considered carefully alongside salary. For some applicants, a lower salary can be offset by a great benefits package.

Benefits should reflect the library's values. If you tell your staff that you value work-life balance, but only offer a week of vacation, your actions will speak louder than words. If you tell staff that you want employees that reflect all age groups, but do not offer family health insurance, they will doubt your words. Of course, your library's financial situation can play a large role in what you are able to offer.

There are a few different categories of benefits that you should consider:

- Health care
- Leave
- Financial
- Other

Consider whether your staff would prefer fewer robust benefits or a larger pool of benefits that are not as comprehensive. For example, you might have really great health insurance but can only offer a small pension benefit. Each decision you make when providing benefits will play into an employee's overall satisfaction and retention.

BENEFITS EQUITY

When determining what benefits to offer, be sure to consider how to make your benefits equitable. Benefits should be consistent across similar job duties and positions. You can offer different benefits packages to staff based on the number of hours they are budgeted to work or based on their position.

When crafting your benefits, consider your own unconscious bias. Do you offer more paid leave for new mothers vs. new fathers? Does your health insurance cover gender confirmation surgery? Are your benefits more focused on new families? What do you offer staff caring for aging parents? Think about how you can support employees at every stage of their life.

Sometimes your benefits themselves might not be an issue, but the way they are implemented may be discriminatory. Do you have different insurance coverage for same sex couples and heterosexual couples regarding fertility treatments?

But be sure to look at the entirety of your benefit offerings and procedures to ensure your decisions are not unintentionally discriminatory.

HEALTH CARE BENEFITS

The first category of benefits to offer is health care benefits, which can range from medical insurance to wellness initiatives.

Medical Insurance

Medical insurance is typically the benefit most staff are interested in. What type of plan you offer and from what insurance carrier should be considered carefully to ensure the highest benefit to staff for the most reasonable cost. In some states, there may be specific guidelines for what you must offer and what employees should pay. Check with your state statutes to determine what the requirements are.

When considering what type of insurance to offer, try to offer family coverage for employees. This is an important benefit not only for families with children but for older employees who might have a spouse retire and want to add them on the insurance.

Some employees may opt out of insurance coverage and ask for a higher salary. But if they have a qualifying life event, they may decide to go back on the insurance. Your safest option is not to offer them higher pay since you cannot predict the future.

Dental Insurance

Typically paired with medical insurance, dental insurance is not as expensive so consider whether you can offer family coverage. If you do offer family coverage, the library may choose to pay more toward single coverage than family coverage. But even covering 50 percent of family coverage is a plus.

Vision Insurance

While many medical insurance plans offer some type of vision discount coverage, having separate vision insurance will provide employees with more comprehensive coverage for exams, glasses, and contacts at a lower cost. These plans are relatively inexpensive for the library and employee, but can yield significant savings for your staff.

Employee Assistance Program (EAP)

Often paired with another insurance plan, EAPs offer confidential counseling services for employees. According to the World Health Organization[2], one in four people will be affected by a mental illness during their lives. EAPs offer free or reduced-cost counseling services and usually have mental health seminars and articles that they send out to employees monthly. Employees typically do not pay for this benefit.

Life Insurance

While pension plans can offer some type of life insurance, offering an additional life insurance plan to employees will give them peace of mind in the event something happens to them. Depending on your library's financial situation, you can pay 100 percent of the premium or have the employee share in some of the cost.

Flex Spending Account (FSA)

FSAs allow employees to set aside pre-tax money to pay for qualified health and/or dependent care expenses. Generally, the money in an FSA must be used within the plan year or you may offer a grace period of up to two and a half extra months. At the end of the year or grace period, unused money is lost.

Health Savings Account (HSA)

HSAs are specific to a high-deductible PPO, meaning deductibles that are higher than the average PPO deductible. With an HSA, employees put money into an account pre-tax and use the funds to pay for health care expenses. The balance in a health savings account can be rolled over each year (unlike an FSA) and go with the employee when they change jobs or leave the workforce.

Health Reimbursement Account (HRA)

While not common in libraries, HRAs are another benefit that can assist staff with health care costs. Unlike an HSA, HRAs are funded by the employer and can be used by the employee to pay for health care expenses including insurance. An HRA can be used in conjunction with or instead of medical insurance.

Wellness Initiatives

Some employers offer wellness initiatives to employees like a discount at a gym, meditation classes, health screenings, or on-site flu shots.

LEAVE BENEFITS

After offering your employees health care benefits, the next most sought after benefit is time off. These benefits range from vacation to medical leaves.

Bereavement Leave

Paid bereavement leave for the death of an immediate family member is a low-cost benefit that everyone should offer.

Disability

If an employee becomes disabled because of sickness or accident and is unable to work on a short-term basis, disability coverage will provide the employee with a certain percentage of their pay for a certain amount of time.

Family Medical Leave Act (FMLA)

FMLA requires eligible employers to provide up to twelve weeks of unpaid job-protected leave for qualifying reasons. This leave can be taken consecutively or intermittently and is only available to employees who have worked for your library for at least twelve months and have at least 1,250 hours of service in the twelve months before taking leave. FMLA is often paired with paid leave.

General Leave of Absence

Sometimes an employee will not qualify for FMLA coverage or your library is not required to offer FMLA leave, but you can still offer them an unpaid (or paid) leave of absence to ensure they can get time off to take care of major life challenges.

Holidays

Most libraries are closed on certain days of the year. Offer holiday pay to full- and part-time staff regularly scheduled to work that day; if you are not giving your employee the option to work, you should pay them when the library is closed.

Paid Parental and Caregiver Leave

Many libraries are now offering paid parental leave to parents of newborns, newly adopted children, or children newly placed into their foster care. Rather than offering only paid parental leave, consider also offering paid leave for those employees who need to take time off to care for aging parents. These leaves are usually used in tandem with FMLA leave.

Paid Time Off (PTO)

Some libraries may offer vacation, sick, and personal days as one bank of paid time off. In some states, government employees can apply sick leave to their pension fund to add time to their years of service. In those instances, having a PTO policy will mean that employees cannot apply that credit.

When thinking about what benefits to offer staff, remember that part-time staff deserve time off as well. While many organizations don't offer part-time staff any paid time off, this trend is changing and more and more organizations are starting to offer at least sick time and often some vacation time to staff. Offering PTO to part-time staff lets those staff members know that you recognize that their health and well-being are important to the organization.

When allocating PTO, have employees accrue PTO on a per-pay-period basis instead of in one lump sum. This will ensure that employees can build up their banks over time. If the employee leaves after a short time and you have provided them with their full year of leave, you may need to pay it all out. Accruing per pay period provides benefits for the employees and employer.

Vacation

Vacation time often comes in right under medical insurance in terms of employee interest. Most libraries will offer different levels of vacation time depending on how many hours employees work or what their pay grade is in the organization. In most libraries, employees will be granted additional vacation time after a certain number of years of service.

One way to make vacation time more equitable is to eliminate the six- or twelve-month waiting period before people may use it.

Sick Leave

Employers can send someone who is sick home, but many do not. According to the CDC, employers lose $1,685 per employee per year in lost productivity.[3] Giving staff sick leave and then reinforcing the policy by encouraging people to stay home when ill will result in fewer people infecting others in the workplace. Don't just offer sick leave to certain employees; offer it to everyone to ensure that they can take time off when they are ill. There are some states where sick pay is mandated so check your local laws to determine if that is true in your state.

Personal Days

In addition to vacation and sick leave, some employers provide personal days to be used for personal business that cannot be accomplished during non-working time.

Voting Leave

Many states have requirements for employers to grant paid leave to vote. Even if your state does not require this, encouraging people to vote and giving them paid time to do it is a smart idea.

FINANCIAL BENEFITS

Employers can offer employees financial incentives beyond their paycheck.

Pension

A pension is a fund that the employer puts money into for an employee's retirement. There are penalties if money is removed early and employees must contribute for a certain number of years in order to be eligible to receive a pension at retirement.

Retirement Savings

Often used in addition to a pension fund, some libraries offer 457 plans, which are the governmental equivalent of a 401(k). Employees who elect to participate in the plan contribute pre-tax to the fund each paycheck and can begin taking it out again after retirement except in some cases where there is an unforeseeable emergency.

Credit Union

These member-owned financial institutions are run by their participants. Libraries may be part of a credit union with other libraries, independently, or with other units of local government. They provide traditional banking services, oftentimes with better rates than a traditional bank.

Tuition Reimbursement

Supporting employees who are going back to school to obtain additional training and credentials will help with your employee retention. Previously, the standard had been to offer some reimbursement in return for the employee guaranteeing to stay for a certain length of time, but that has shifted to offering smaller reimbursements without the requirement to stay at the library.

OTHER BENEFITS

Commuter/Parking Benefits

Commuter benefits allow the employee to set aside pre-tax money to pay for qualified transportation expenses. If your employees take mass transit (bus/train/subway) to work or pay to park, this benefit is very beneficial as it allows them to significantly reduce their commuting expenses.

Remote Work

With the COVID-19 pandemic, remote work went from a benefit to a necessity. We still do not know the long-term impacts the pandemic will have on remote work, but having a remote work benefit for people is advised.

Professional Development

As institutions of lifelong learning, we should provide our staff with access to professional development so they can be lifelong learners. While this is listed in the benefits section, this should never be something that is eliminated from your benefits package. We will talk more about the need for professional development in chapter 7 (Continual Training and Career Development).

Professional Memberships

For staff who work in certain positions, offering professional memberships to trade associations will ensure they can stay connected in their field. Libraries often focus on librarians, but other staff in your organization could also benefit:

- Business managers/ accountants
- HR
- IT
- Marketing
- Graphics
- Programming
- Makerspaces

TOTAL COMPENSATION PACKAGE

Now that you have presented the new hire with a salary and benefits package, they can evaluate what you are offering as a whole. In the offer letter, make sure to list not only the salary but also the full benefits package they will receive.

Consider providing staff members with a total compensation breakdown and cost for each benefit annually (see table 3.2 for an example).

HR LAW

When considering how to craft a compensation package for employees, there are federal and state laws that you need to be aware of.

FAIR LABOR STANDARDS ACT (FLSA)

The FLSA is a law passed in 1938 that provides certain rights to employees. States may have more specific laws that will apply.

Minimum Wage

This establishes a federal minimum wage, but many states have passed laws that increase the minimum wage in the state. Employers are required to pay employees at or above the minimum wage. Some states have a higher minimum wage but allow for the federal minimum wage for workers under eighteen.

Overtime

The FLSA establishes who is eligible for overtime and how that overtime must be calculated. The Department of Labor has a Fact Sheet that provides more information on determining who is exempt from overtime regulations: www.dol.gov.

TABLE 3.2 | **Total compensation package**

FULL-TIME LIBRARIAN		35 HOUR WORKWEEK	
SALARY AND LEAVE	HOURS	ANNUAL	HOURLY
Salary	1820	$50,000	$27.47
Salary includes:			
Vacation	160	$4,395.60	
Sick	80	$2,197.80	
Holidays	80	$2,197.80	
Personal	16	$439.56	
Bereavement	24	$659.34	
Remote Work	364	$ -	
Total		$50,000	
HEALTHCARE	YOUR COST	LIBRARY COST	DESCRIPTION
Medical	$1,175.64	$10,580.28	PPO Single Coverage
Dental	$47.76	$429.48	PPO Single Coverage
Vision	$8.64	$429.48	Single Coverage
Life	$ -		$67,500 in Coverage
Total	$1,232.04	$11,439.24	
RETIREMENT	YOUR COST	LIBRARY COST	
Pension Contributions	$2,250.00	$2,250.00	
FICA	$3,825.00	$3,825.00	
457	$5,000.00	$ -	
Total	$11,075.00	$6,075.00	
OTHER BENEFITS	YOUR COST	LIBRARY COST	
Professional Development	$ -	$500.00	
Professional Memberships	$ -	$500.00	
Total	$ -	$1,000.00	
TOTAL COMPENSATION			
Salary	$50,000.00		
Healthcare	$11,439.24		
Retirement	$6,075.00		
Other	$1,000.00		
TOTAL	$68,514.24		

Equal Pay Provisions

Gender-based wage differences between employees of opposite genders employed in the same organization who perform jobs that require equal skill, effort, and responsibility are prohibited under the FLSA.

FAMILY MEDICAL LEAVE ACT

FMLA is an unpaid leave and required for any organization with fifty or more employees or is a government agency. Check with your attorney to determine if your library must provide FMLA coverage.

AFFORDABLE CARE ACT (ACA)

The ACA states that employers with fifty or more full-time employees or full-time equivalents based on a thirty-hour workweek are required to provide health care that is affordable and provides minimum value to their employees. Coverage must not exceed a certain percentage of an employee's household income and must be provided to anyone working thirty or more hours per week. There are strict penalties for employers who do not comply.

FEDERAL INSURANCE CONTRIBUTIONS ACT (FICA)

FICA is a federal payroll tax that both employers and employees contribute to in order to fund the Social Security and Medicare programs in the United States. Employers contribute 7.65% per employee and employees pay 7.65% of their pay in FICA taxes from each paycheck, totaling 15.3%.

APPLYING YOUR LEARNING: MINIMUM WAGE

The Anytown Library has a conundrum. The year prior, the state enacted a five-year minimum wage stepping scale to $15/hour. The library has a very tight budget and employs nine people. There are a few employees who make just over $15 per hour and have been at the library for a while, with no wage increase. One is the circulation manager. The remaining under-minimum-wage staff will be receiving the step increases annually to keep them in step with the new minimum wage law. However, with the limited budget this means that the other staff will not receive any wage increase.

The staff who received the increase were in the circulation department. Once they reached $15 per hour, their manager was making just a bit more than their staff, and had worked at the library for over six years. She asked the library director for a $4.50 per hour wage increase to be more in line with the other circulation managers in the area. The library director said that it was not possible to increase her wage. The circulation manager found employment at a neighboring library for $20/hour.

QUESTIONS

1. What is the primary issue in this scenario?
2. Who are the players involved?
3. What went well in how this was handled?
4. What should have been handled differently? Why?
5. What laws might come into play on this topic?
6. How would you have approached handling this scenario?

KEY TAKEAWAYS

A total compensation package includes two parts—salary and benefits. The package should be reflective of a library's compensation philosophy and financial reality.

Salaries comprise one part of a total compensation package and should be determined based on a salary schedule that lists the following:

- Position titles
- FLSA status
- Minimum, midpoint, and maximum of the range
- When it went into effect
- How many hours per week for full-time

Once the schedule is completed, you need to determine how to implement it and what impact it will have on your library's budget.

The other part of a compensation package is benefits, which include health care, leaves, financial benefits, and other benefits.

Health Care
- Medical insurance (HMO, PPO)
- Dental insurance
- Vision insurance
- Employee Assistance Program
- Life insurance

- – FSA
- – HSA
- – HRA
- Wellness initiatives

Leaves
- Bereavement
- Disability
- FMLA
- General leave of absence
- Holidays
- Paid parental and caregiver leave
- Paid time off (vacation, sick, personal)
- Voting

Financial
- Pension
- Retirement savings
- Credit union
- Tuition reimbursement

Other Benefits
- Commuter/parking benefits
- Remote work
- Professional development
- Professional memberships

REFLECTION QUESTIONS FOR CHAPTER 3

- What is my library's compensation philosophy?
- Does my library have a salary schedule that has been updated in the last three to five years?
- What unique benefits do we offer employees?
- Are my benefits equitable and do we offer options for staff at different stages of life?
- Do we regularly share with staff what their total compensation is?

ADDITIONAL RESOURCES

American Library Association. "Library Salaries Information." December 2015. www.ala.org/educationcareers/employment/salaries.

American Library Association Allied Professional Association. "ALA-APA Library Salary Database." https://ala-apa.org/improving-salariesstatus/resources/ala-apa-librarian-and-library-worker-salary-surveys/.

Employee Benefits Security Administration. "Affordable Care Act." U.S. Department of Labor. www.dol.gov/agencies/ebsa/laws-and-regulations/laws/affordable-care-act.

O*NET Online by U.S. Department of Labor. www.onetonline.org.

U.S. Wage and Hour Division. "Family and Medical Leave Act." U.S. Department of Labor. www.dol.gov/agencies/whd/fmla.

U.S. Wage and Hour Division. "State Minimum Wage Laws." U.S. Department of Labor. www.dol.gov/agencies/whd/minimum-wage/state.

NOTES

1. Elise Silva and Quinn Galbraith, "Salary Negotiation Patterns between Women and Men in Academic Libraries," *College and Research Libraries* 79, no. 3 (2018), https://crl.acrl.org/index.php/crl/article/view/16689/18646.

2. World Health Organization, "The World Health Report 2001: Mental Disorders Affect One in Four People," news release, September 28, 2001, www.who.int/news/item/28-09-2001-the-world-health-report-2001-mental-disorders-affect-one-in-four-people.

3. Center for Disease Control and Prevention, "Worker Productivity Measures," April 1, 2016, www.cdc.gov/workplacehealthpromotion/model/evaluation/productivity.html.

CHAPTER 4

Onboarding

After reading this chapter you will know the following:

+ What key HR tasks to do on the employee's first day
+ How to set your new employee up for success
+ What HR laws you and new employees need to know

||||||||||||||||||||||||||||||||||||||||||||||||||||||||||||||||||||||||||||||||||||||||||||||||||||||||||||||||||||||||||||||||||||||||||||||||||

Congratulations! Your new employee is about to start, and it is time to think about onboarding. Depending on their position, training may take a few months to a full year, and creating an onboarding checklist will ensure that nothing is missed. You can find a sample onboarding checklist in the Toolkit.

FIRST DAY

Prior to the employee's first day, reach out to them with an email or call. Express your excitement to have them join your team. Confirm their start date and time, tell them which door to come to, and let them know any documents they need to bring. Make sure to share what the dress code is and ask if they have any other questions before they arrive.

FROM THE DIRECTOR'S CORNER—KATE'S STORY

I have worked at six different libraries thus far in my career. For me, the most nerve-wracking part of a new job is the first day. I have high anxiety when I have to navigate a new system, and there are so many things to be anxious about on your first day: what to wear, when to leave home, whether to bring a lunch, what door to go in. My anxiety would continue inflating until that critical first day was over. Today I couldn't tell you what I did on any of my first days, but I can vividly remember the anxiety I felt leading up to them.

MORAL: Make sure new staff know what to do, where to go, and any other info that will make their first day less stressful.

On their first day, designate someone to greet them at the door. Then, it's time to get started on the paperwork. If you decide to send them the required paperwork ahead of time, remember that the time the employee spends filling out the paperwork must be recorded on their timesheet and paid.

There are required federal and state forms, in addition to any library-specific forms they will need to fill out:

- W-4 and state tax forms (must be completed before first paycheck is issued)
- I-9 form (must be completed within three days of their start date)
- Benefit forms such as medical, dental, and life insurance (they may fill this out later)
- Emergency contact form
- Name tag form (if you didn't get this as part of their acceptance information)
- Direct deposit form (review when and how people are paid and remember that you cannot require someone to do direct deposit)
- Employee handbook and acknowledgment form (generally they take this, read the handbook, and return the signed form later)

Some staff may not go by their legal name or may want to use a nickname on their name tag. Laws often lag behind current practice and the employee may still have to put their legal name on official forms. But you should check with staff on what they want listed for:

- Name tags
- Email
- Business cards
- Staff directory

Adding pronouns (she/her, he/him, they/their, ze/hir) will send a strong message about where your library is on its inclusion journey.

During this time, you also want to provide them with the following information and items:

- Keys or access codes
- Computer login and email address
- Telephone instructions for setting up voice mail, answering calls, transferring, and so on
- Parking instructions or permits (if needed)
- Break and meal guidelines
- Timesheets or clocking in/out
- Organizational chart
- Job description

Providing branded library items like a mug or notebook to new staff is another way to welcome them.

DEALING WITH THE PAPERWORK

What do you do with all the paperwork needed for each employee? When setting up your HR files, have separate employee files for the following:
- I-9 binder, which has the I-9s for everyone in the organization
- Medical/ ADA folder for any employee who receives an accommodation, FMLA, or other leave, or has an injury and workers' compensation claim at work
- Personnel file includes the new hire paperwork, evaluations, kudos from staff or patrons, and disciplinary warnings.

If you currently have all the files together, work on a plan to separate them. You are required by law to keep the I-9s separate and should keep any medical/ADA information separate as well.

Once the paperwork is completed, take them to their new department and work area. If they have their own work space, make sure it has been prepared for them and stocked with basic supplies. Keep in mind that they will be inundated with information during the first few days. Assume that they will not remember everything and only go over the basics.

- Take them on a tour of the library, focusing on their work areas and department.
- Help them set up their email, voice mail, and any other technology setup and share where to go with IT issues.

- Introduce them to staff and assign a departmental buddy. This person should be someone whom the new employee can go to with questions and help the new employee get to know the culture of the library and the unwritten norms that exist in the organization.
- Share how to access internal documents and files, making sure they can access documents and other tools in it. Highlight online training videos or procedures.
- Review collaboration tools like Slack, Trello, GChat, Basecamp, Jabber, and so on.

When it is time for lunch, offer to take them to lunch. Some may find that more harrowing than fun and may just want to take the break by themselves. Your actions should be guided by your employee's reaction to your offer. If you do go out, invite their buddy and make sure not to talk about work.

After lunch, give them time alone to get their bearings and look through everything, but let them know how to get in touch with you or their department buddy with any questions.

FIRST WEEK

During the first week, share a training checklist with them with topics and deadlines. Every employee needs to be an active participant in their learning journey. Don't assume that just because they worked at another library they don't need to be trained on your library's procedures.

Take time to introduce the new employee to everyone else in the department. Perhaps you have them shadow others or just do a quick meet and greet. Your job is to help them learn about the culture and values of the library and assist them in getting to know other staff members. The department buddy you assigned to them will also help.

CREATING A WELCOMING AND INCLUSIVE CULTURE

Employees come to the workplace with many different identities. To create a welcoming and inclusive culture, consider how someone's identities impact how they experience the workplace. Often, only certain identities such as white able-bodied women are centered and normalized.

- Pronounce an employee's name correctly. If you can't remember, ask them politely to repeat it, but don't modify someone's name for your comfort. Consider creating a phonetic name directory with recordings of everyone saying their name.

- Acknowledge where your organization is at in your equity, diversity, and inclusion (EDI) journey. If your library hasn't done any EDI work previously, acknowledge it and talk about what steps you are taking now.
- Introduce new employees with their position and accomplishments. Share some of the talents new staff bring to the table. This will also make new staff feel appreciated for what they are bringing to the organization.
- Model psychological and emotional safety. Psychological safety, as coined by Harvard's Dr. Amy Edmonson, is "a belief that you will not be punished or humiliated for speaking up with ideas, questions, concerns or mistakes." Modeling it means taking risks, learning from failures, and actively seeking ideas that are different from your own.

Go over their job description in detail with them and give them a list of what they will be responsible for in their role. Having a list of who does what in each department is beneficial not only for new employees, but for staff in the department.

Once they are clear on their responsibilities, share a "Key Days and Dates" list with the employee so they can start building their calendar. The list should include important department and/or library dates:

- All staff meetings
- Department meetings
- One-on-one meetings with manager (typically every two to four weeks)
- Staff trainings including staff development days
- Team building events (holiday gatherings, staff potlucks, etc.)
- Closing dates
- Key programs throughout the year (e.g., summer reading)
- Outreach events (include only if they are asked to participate)
- Evaluations
- Budget planning (depending on position)
- Regional, state, and national conferences (also include who the library can send and how that works)
- Any other special meetings they might be required to participate in (e.g., meetings with all the programmers or collection development specialists, etc.)

- Other (think about other things that someone in that position needs to be aware of in terms of when things happen, like newsletter deadlines)

Check in daily with the employee if you are not the one doing their training. Be sure there is a system to answer questions. Perhaps you prefer they ask you questions as soon as something pops up, or maybe you prefer to have them hold all the questions until a weekly one-on-one meeting. You need to be aware of what your preferred communication style is and then communicate that to the employee. Determining communication styles will be covered in chapter 6 (Feedback and Evaluation).

Toward the end of their first week, have your first one-on-one meeting. When the employee is still being trained, consider meeting weekly with them and then move to semiweekly or monthly over time. Use your first meeting to get to know the employee's work and communication style, lay out expectations, and learn what you can do to help them succeed in their new role. Prepare an agenda in advance and share it with the employee so they can have comments and/or questions prepared. Some sample topics are:

JOB DUTIES

- Review the job description and go over the specific job duties they will have.
- Lay out your expectations for what success in this role looks like.

MOTIVATION AND FEEDBACK

- What motivates them to succeed?
- How do they like to receive recognition (public/private)?
- How have they received feedback from managers in the past? Do they have a preferred way of receiving feedback?

GOALS

- What are their short-, medium-, and long-term career goals?
- What projects are they hoping to work on in their role?

TRAINING AND DEVELOPMENT

- What skills or knowledge do they want to build?
- What would make these one-on-one meetings the most valuable for them?

- What does success look like in their first thirty days?
- Tell them what you think success looks like in their first thirty days.

COMMUNICATION

- Review how you and your team communicate.
- What is their preferred method of communicating (phone, email, etc.)?
- What questions do they have and how should they follow up if they have a question later?

This first meeting will not only give you valuable insight into your new employee, but will also give you an opportunity to lay out clear expectations and share more about how you manage. Check in from time to time with their department buddy and see what else you can do to help the new employee succeed.

FIRST QUARTER

Within the first three months, the employee should become more comfortable in their role. During this period, continue to meet regularly with them and have their department buddy check in with them. When you meet, have a set agenda that you and the employee both follow:

- How did the last week go? What immediate questions or concerns do they have?
- Follow up on challenges that they mentioned at the last one-on-one to see if those are resolved or still need discussion.

TRAINING FOLLOW-UP

- What questions do they have on the training they completed?
- What is one thing they have learned from their training since the last meeting?
- Go over the next training topics.

FEEDBACK

- What has worked well with the training?
- Is there anything in the department or library that they feel could be improved?

- Offer the employee feedback on how they have done. Be specific and make sure the feedback focuses on the positive ways they are performing.

SUPPORT

- What can you do to support them until your next meeting?

NEXT STEPS

- What action steps do they need to take based on today's conversation?
- What action steps do you need to take based on today's conversation?

While most employees will perform well in their new role, some may not. If you are finding that they are experiencing issues learning their job, make sure you have clearly communicated your expectations for their role and ensure they have completed the training that will give them the tools they need to succeed. When you have a new employee who is not performing at the level you would expect after a few months and you have given them clear expectations and the necessary training, consider whether they are able to succeed in the position. It is better to act early, even if that means terminating someone, than to let an employee who cannot perform the job stay on because you do not want to deal with the issue directly. We will cover the issue of discipline and termination in chapter 11.

Once the employee has the basic tasks down, you can start working with them on departmental and library-wide procedures. You may have shared some of the information with them on the first day, but it will help to go over it with them again:

TRAINING AND DEVELOPMENT

- How do they request continuing education (CE) or professional development (PD) training?
- How do they get reimbursed for travel/meal expenses?
- Are professional memberships paid for by the organization?

EMERGENCY PROCEDURES

- Where is the emergency manual?
- What training is offered to staff on emergencies?
- Go over basic emergency training with them (fire alarm, power outage, weather, etc.).
- Take them on a tour of the building to show them where exits, fire extinguishers, and any other important areas or things are located.

FINANCES

- Go over the budget lines they need to be aware of or are in charge of (programming, supplies, collections, etc.).
- Explain how ordering works for the different lines.
- Give them a high-level overview of how the library is funded and how the budget is set each year.

REPORTS AND STATISTICS

- Go over where departmental and library-wide statistics are kept.
- Explain how statistics are gathered and used and what, if any, role they have in collecting statistics.
- Share monthly report templates with them and explain what you expect from them in terms of updating you on projects or goals.
- Review how evaluations work and what they should keep track of in order for them to engage in the evaluation process (more on this in chapter 6 [Feedback and Evaluation]).

Depending on the role, some of these may not be covered until after the first quarter or will only need to be covered minimally. With each interaction, look for opportunities to share the library's values, mission, and vision and how it ties into the work that they do on a day-to-day basis.

FIRST YEAR

Within the first year, your employee should be confident in performing their basic job duties and understand how the department operates and how it correlates with other library departments.

Employees should understand what each department does and how each department supports one another. Depending on the number of hours worked each week and their role in the organization, have the new employee spend an hour or two in each department and learn about how that department operates and some of their key tasks. Not only will this allow the employee to get a more top-level view of the library, but it will also help them build relationships outside of their department, which will increase collaboration and reduce departmental silos. Depending on the size of your library, you may also have employees cross-trained in other departments. Wait until the employee is confident in their assigned tasks before starting any cross-training.

Their main goal in year one is learning how to perform the assigned duties. By the end of the first year, this goal should be complete and it will be time for them to start setting ongoing goals. We talk more about goal setting in chapter 6 (Feedback and Evaluation).

By the end of their first year, you can transition to either semimonthly or monthly one-on-one meetings. These meetings will change to focus more on projects and ongoing development. As with your one-on-one meetings, you should have a set agenda for these meetings. Suggested questions and topics are:

- How are things going?
- Go over existing and potential projects (most of this can be summarized in a monthly report, which is a more expedient way to share updates, leaving more time to discuss roadblocks or explore future projects).
- Review goals.
- Provide feedback on projects.
- Are they experiencing any challenges or roadblocks that you can help with?
- What are their priorities for the next month?
- What support do they need from you right now?
- Is there anything else that should be discussed or that they think you should know about?
- What action steps do either of you need to take based on today's conversation?

By the end of the first year, you will have given your employee the expectation, tools, and feedback they need to be successful in their new role.

HR LAW

When onboarding a new employee, there are many laws that you need to be aware of as a manager, but there are also laws that the employee must be cognizant of.

EMPLOYEE POSTING REQUIREMENTS

There are federal and state employee posting requirements that all employers must post in an easily accessible location in each of their physical locations for staff. These posters alert employees to federal and state laws that protect their rights and share information on who they can contact if their employer is not following state or federal laws. The Department of Labor has a FirstStep Poster Advisor,[1] who gives specific requirements by state.

FAIR LABOR STANDARDS ACT (FLSA)

The FLSA is a law passed in 1938 that provides certain rights to employees. States may have more specific laws that will apply.

Nursing Mothers

In 2009, Congress amended the FLSA to require break times for nursing mothers. Employers are required to provide reasonable break times for nursing mothers to express breast milk privately without fear of intrusion. The law protects nursing mothers up to one year from the date of the child's birth and allows the nursing mother to take as many breaks as are needed. The law does not specify what "reasonable" means and you should check with your library attorney to ensure you are not violating the law if this comes up. Designate a location that is not a bathroom for this purpose. Normalizing pumping for nursing mothers helps reduce stigma of women returning to the workforce. The onus on determining where they can pump should not be on the employee, but on the library.

Recordkeeping

The law also requires employers to keep certain information on employees including:

- Personal information including name, address, and so forth
- What hours are worked each day and week
- When the workweek begins
- How much overtime the employee received (if eligible)
- Their rate of pay for straight time earnings and overtime
- Deductions from or additions to their wages
- Total wages paid each period
- When the payment was made to the employee and what dates are covered

Employers must ensure that exempt and nonexempt employees are tracking their work hours each day.

I-9, EMPLOYMENT ELIGIBILITY REQUIREMENT

On the first day of work, the employee must complete Section 1 of the I-9. Within three business days of the date of hire, the employer must complete Sections 2 and 3. Employees must bring in documents from the list of acceptable documents[2] to establish their identity and employment authorization. The form must be kept by the employer and housed separately from the personnel file. If you are unsure whether your library has an I-9 for every employee, you should complete an I-9 audit.

MEAL AND REST BREAKS

While federal law does not require meal breaks or shorter breaks, many states do require unpaid meal breaks. When an employer offers short breaks (typically ten to fifteen minutes), federal law considers that time as compensable. Employers should include the time in determining whether overtime is awarded. Additional breaks or break flexibility may be necessary as an accommodation for religious observance. An employer can always choose to be more generous and also pay for meal breaks, as long as they are doing so consistently throughout the organization.

APPLYING YOUR LEARNING: PARENTAL LEAVE AND NURSING MOTHERS

Brianna had started her new job as a reference librarian the month before. Her training and onboarding had been thorough and, luckily, her morning sickness had already stopped. With only three months until she was due to have twins, she knew it was time to tell her manager.

Her manager congratulated her and then HR went over the parental leave benefits. As she approached her due date, her coworkers held a shower for her and Brianna prepared for being off. Because she had started less than a year before, she was not eligible for FMLA and had used all of her sick time on doctor visits, but the library did provide an unpaid leave of absence.

Six weeks after the birth of her twins, Brianna returned to work. On her first day back, she went to her manager and reminded them that she would need to have breaks to pump. Her manager had forgotten, but after a quick meeting with HR, the manager told her she could pump in the women's restroom. They would just put a sign up while she was in there telling people not to go inside.

Brianna didn't want to pump in a restroom, but she didn't think she had a choice. After a few weeks of this, Brianna asked to work part-time and did for a few more months before deciding that this wasn't going to work for her.

At her exit interview, when asked why she was leaving, Brianna told HR that it was too hard to work with twins. What she didn't say out loud was that she felt uncomfortable pumping in the women's restroom. HR never learned what the real problem was.

QUESTIONS

1. What is the primary issue in this scenario?
2. Who are the players involved?
3. What went well in how this was handled?
4. What should have been handled differently? Why?
5. What laws might come into play on this topic?
6. How would you have approached handling this scenario?

KEY TAKEAWAYS

Onboarding your employee begins before they start and will last through their first year. On the first day, make sure they fill out the required paperwork:

- W-4 and state tax forms
- I-9 form
- Benefit forms such as medical, dental, and life insurance

Onboarding is about more than just teaching someone the ins and outs of their job; it is also about creating a welcoming and inclusive environment. Having a training schedule and plan will help with the onboarding, while having a library buddy for the new employee will help them feel welcome.

REFLECTION QUESTIONS FOR CHAPTER 4

- How have I onboarded staff in the past? What worked and what didn't?
- Does my library have onboarding checklists for new employees for HR, departmental, and job-specific onboarding?
- How do we convey our library's culture to new employees?
- What are we doing to make new staff feel welcomed on their first day, week, month, and year?
- Are we complying with all applicable labor laws?

ADDITIONAL RESOURCES

HR360. "Meals and Rest Breaks in All 50 States." www.hr360.com/statelaws/
Connecticut/Meal-and-Rest-Breaks-in-All-50-States.aspx.

Bevegni, Stephanie (Howell). *Onboarding in a Box*. LinkedIn Talent Solutions.
https://business.linkedin.com/content/dam/business/talent-solutions/
global/en_us/c/pdfs/onboarding-in-a-box-v03-06.pdf.

Maurer, Roy. "New Employee Onboarding Guide." SHRM, www.shrm.org/resources
andtools/hr-topics/talent-acquisition/pages/new-employee-onboarding
-guide.aspx.

Society for Human Resources Management. "How to Conduct an I-9 Audit." SHRM
How-To Guides. www.shrm.org/resourcesandtools/tools-and-samples/
how-to-guides/pages/conductani-9audit.aspx.

Society for Human Resources Management. "I-9 Audit Checklist." https://www
.shrm.org/resourcesandtools/tools-and-samples/hr-forms/pages/i-9
auditchecklist.aspx

Society for Human Resources Management. "Managing the Employee Onboarding
and Assimilation Process." www.shrm.org/resourcesandtools/tools-and
-samples/toolkits/pages/onboardingandassimilationprocess.aspx.

U.S. Citizenship and Immigration Services. "Guidance for Employers Conducting
Form I-9 Audits." www.uscis.gov/i-9-central/form-i-9-related-news/
guidance-for-employers-conducting-form-i-9-audits.

U.S. Citizenship and Immigration Services. "I-9, Employment Eligibility Verifica-
tion." https://www.uscis.gov/i-9.

U.S. Department of Labor. "Breaks and Meal Periods." www.dol.gov/general/topic/
workhours/breaks.

U.S. Department of Labor. "FirstStep Poster Advisor." https://webapps.dol.gov/
elaws/posters.htm.

U.S. Department of Labor. "Handy Reference Guide to the Fair Labor Standards
Act." Wage and Honor Division. www.dol.gov/agencies/whd/compliance
-assistance/handy-reference-guide-flsa.

U.S. Department of Labor. "Minimum Length of Meal Period Required under State
Law for Adult Employees in Private Sector 1." www.dol.gov/agencies/whd/
state/meal-breaks.

U.S. Department of Labor. "State Labor Offices." www.dol.gov/agencies/whd/state/
contacts.

NOTES

1. U.S. Department of Labor, "*FirstStep* Poster Advisor," https://webapps.dol.gov/elaws/posters.htm?_ga=2.265419404.249328431.1607139974-220671112.1607139974.

2. U.S. Citizenship and Immigration Services, "Form I-9 Acceptable Documents," www.uscis.gov/i-9-central/acceptable-documents.

CHAPTER 5

Personnel Policies and Procedures

After reading this chapter you will know the following:
+ How to tell the difference between policies and procedures
+ What key personnel policies you should have for your library
+ How to write an effective policy
+ How to write clear procedures

||||||||||||||||||||||||||||||||||||||||||||||||||||||||||||||||||||||||||||||||||||||||||||||||||||||||||||||||||||||||

Personnel policies are approved by the board and lay out expectations and provide key information to staff. Procedures are the instructions for staff on how to complete different processes within the library and are not approved by the board. Policies and procedures are not the same, but they do work in conjunction with each other.

POLICIES

There are three main purposes for personnel policies:

1. To provide benefits information
2. To provide a framework for employers and employees to set expectations
3. To comply with state and federal law

CREATING AND REVIEWING PERSONNEL POLICIES

Most libraries will already have an existing personnel policy or employee handbook, and creating one from scratch will not be necessary. However, it may be missing policies that will need to be created. In some instances, the library might be required to follow a city/village/township/county personnel policy. In other instances, if some workers are part of a union, certain policies will be laid out as part of the union contract. The full personnel policy should be reviewed thoroughly at least every three to five years, but individual policies may change more frequently based on new laws or changes in benefits offered.

Start a List of Needed Policies

Begin by cross-checking your current policy manual against the sample personnel policy list below. When reviewing the list, mark any policies that you feel you should add to your manual. Check with your state library or library attorney on what policies are required in your state. See figure 5.1 for a list of recommended policies.

REVIEW EXISTING POLICIES

Before creating the new policies, review and update the existing policies. Your library's mission, vision, and value statements, in addition to the compensation philosophy discussed in chapter 3 (Salary and Benefits), will guide the update of the existing policies and the creation of any new ones. If your library has a union, review the union contract and ensure that any policy updates are consistent with that document. Begin by reading through and marking any obvious changes to your existing policies. Look for items that are no longer accurate or that don't reflect your library's vision and values.

Once you have marked up your existing manual with basic changes, gather sample policies from other libraries to see how they have treated the subject. Look at libraries in your area, of similar size, and out of state to get a wide range and then create a list of the libraries that have policies that would be the best match. A copy of the Northbrook (Illinois) Public Library's Employee Handbook is available on our website.[1] While libraries share freely, the downside to using other libraries' policies is a) the wording can become inconsistent with your other policies and b) the policies may not have been reviewed by an attorney. *Employee* may be used in one policy, *staff member* in the next. Remember to change the wording when borrowing policies to be consistent with the terminology used in your policies.

Create New Policies

Once the existing policies are updated, the rest will have to be created. When writing a policy, start by asking the following questions:

FIGURE 5.1 | **Recommended policies**

GUIDELINES	BENEFITS	CONDUCT
• Americans with Disability Act (ADA)/reasonable accommodations • Attendance • Bloodborne pathogens/exposure control plan • Compensation (pay periods and payroll deductions) • Compensatory time (overtime) • Dress guidelines • Employment-at-will (if at-will state) • Employment eligibility • Employment status and Fair Labor Standards Act classification • Equal Employment Opportunity • Identity protection • Meal and rest breaks • Open door communication policy • Performance evaluations • Personnel records (confidentiality of information) • Progressive discipline • Reimbursable expenses • Selection of personnel (authority to hire, reference and background checks, conflict of interest/nepotism) • Termination of employment • Timesheet recording • Wage and salary guidelines • Workweek	• Bereavement leave • Commuter benefits • Continuation of health coverage (COBRA) • Emergency closings • Employee Assistance Program (EAP) • Family Medical Leave Act (FMLA) • Flexible spending accounts (health and dependent care coverage) • Health savings accounts • Holidays and library closings • Insurance (dental, health, life, vision, and unemployment) • Jury and witness duty • Leaves of absence • Military leave • Paid caregiver leave • Pensions • Professional memberships • Remote work • Short-term and long-term disability • Sick leave • Staff library card • Training and development • Tuition reimbursement • Vacation • Voting time • Workers' compensation	• Anti-bullying • Cell phone usage • Credit card usage • Drug- and alcohol-free workplace • No solicitation/no distribution • Non-discrimination and anti-harassment • Personal vehicle • Smoke-free workplace • Standards of conduct • Technology and social media • Travel • Whistleblower compliance

- What is the purpose of this policy?
- What is the scope of this policy?
- Who is the audience for this policy?
- Are there any other similar policies already in existence?
- Is this too vague to enforce?
- Is this policy being written because of the actions of one employee or a very small group of employees?
- Is this policy consistent with how the library wants to treat employees based on the library's mission, vision, and values?

Policies exist as a guide for library staff and managers to help them understand what the expectations of working at the library are. Once these questions are answered, don't immediately start writing the policy; look at the sample policies gathered from other libraries to determine if there are parts that could be incorporated into the policy.

After reviewing policies from other libraries and marking sections that will work in the policy you are drafting, start writing your policy. To help maintain consistency, create a policy template that can be used for each new policy:

- Type of policy (general, collection, personnel)
- Policy section (e.g., guidelines, benefits, conduct)
- Policy name (may also include a number for easy reference)
- Policy creation date (when the board approves the policy)
- Policy update dates (any time a policy is updated and reviewed by the board)
- Purpose of policy (if needed)
- Policy

Put each policy on a separate page. When it is time to update the policies, having one per page will make it easier to update all manuals.

To create the most effective policies, keep these tips in mind:

Keep it simple: Keep the purpose of the policy at the forefront. Don't add in every possibility to the policy. Remember this is a guiding document, not a comprehensive training manual for every situation.

Be concise: Don't create a three-page policy when a three-paragraph policy will suffice. Make sure it is easy to scan and glean the main points.

Avoid acronyms and initialisms: Not everyone is familiar with library or legal terms. Remember to write everything out so people reading the policies know what you are talking about.

Be consistent: Having a style manual for common words used is helpful (staff *member* vs. *employee*, etc.).

Revise when necessary: Go back and revise if there are policies that don't work as originally intended. Policies should be living documents that change as the library's needs change.

Once the new policies are created, read through it again (Draft 2), looking for inconsistencies and gaps.

FROM THE DIRECTOR'S CORNER—KATE'S STORY

Just like when writing a general policy for patrons, generally avoid writing a policy because of one person's actions. However, there are exceptions to that rule, as I experienced as a new director:

The board hired me to come in and make significant changes quickly. One of the longtime managers went to the board president and told them I was ruining the library and making staff miserable.

The board president alerted me immediately. After speaking with the manager and resolving the issues, I recognized that clearer guidance for myself and the board was needed to ensure these situations were handled appropriately. And so, the open-door communication policy was created.

It gave staff a clear path to air grievances and gave managers, the board, and me a system on how to handle those grievances, ensuring that the role of the board and director did not get blurred.

MORAL: Communication is hard. Clear guidelines can help.

Internal Review

Once the manual is updated and new policies crafted, share it with key staff. Ask them to review the manual:

- Are there any grammatical errors or inconsistent language?
- Is the policy clear and enforceable?
- Does the policy align with the mission, vision, and values?
- Are there any unwritten, unspoken, but understood policies that need to be added?

Once the key staff have provided feedback, update the policy again and read through it (Draft 3).

Expert Review

Once the staff review is completed, turn it over to the experts. Ideally you will have not only an HR attorney review it, but also an equity, diversity, and inclusion (EDI) consultant. While having the attorney review the policy might seem like an unnecessary expense, it can save major headaches down the road and help to avoid having any policies that do not comply with local, state, or federal law. There will also be times when a law changes and a policy may need to be revised before a review of the full policy manual. If the library has an attorney that specializes in libraries and/or municipal law or human resources, they should keep you up to date on any changes to laws that require new policies and will also often provide a sample policy.

When creating or updating a personnel policy manual, there are some policies that you are legally required to have from a federal perspective and some that may be required from your state. The attorney that reviews your policies will tell you about any legally required policies. Listed below are a few policies to make sure you include in your personnel policy manual:

- Guidelines
  - Americans with Disability Act (ADA)/reasonable accommodations
  - Bloodborne pathogens/exposure control plan
  - Compensatory time (overtime)
  - Equal Employment Opportunity
  - Employment status and Fair Labor Standards Act classification
  - Personnel records (confidentiality of information)

- Benefits
  - Continuation of health coverage (COBRA)
  - Family Medical Leave Act (FMLA) (if you have over fifty FTEs)
  - Military leave
  - Workers' compensation

- Conduct
  - Drug- and alcohol-free workplace
  - Non-discrimination and anti-harassment
  - Whistleblower compliance

After reviewing changes from the attorney (Draft 4), if you have the opportunity, have an EDI consultant review it. Creating an equitable organization means making sure your library reflects the backgrounds and abilities of all your employees. The personnel policy is the best place to start. It should be one of the first introductions to the library new employees will have before training on anything else.

If you are unable to hire an outside consultant, assess the policy manual through an equity lens by reviewing the wording, looking over defining statements, and checking your assumptions.

Wording
- Use gender-neutral language
- Be consistent in defining populations listed in the policies: race, creed, color, national origin, religion, marital status, sexual orientation, gender, gender identity/expression, physical appearance, socioeconomic level, education level, and any other legally protected characteristics
- Consider the staff reading it. Will staff feel represented by the language used?

Defining Statements
- Use the policy manual as an opportunity to reflect the library's values.
- Provide an equity statement at the start of the manual.
- Consider the staff reading it. Will they feel the policies and way they are laid out reflect their lived experiences?

Check Your Assumptions
- Consider the reasoning behind each policy. Does it unfairly target certain genders, races, or other populations?
- Is the policy equitable for staff (e.g., maternity leave vs. parental leave vs. caregiver leave)?
- Have you checked your assumptions and created policies that are equitable for all staff?

INTERSECTING IDENTITIES

Our own bias can prevent us from treating others fairly. When crafting a personnel policy, think about the different advantages and disadvantages of the various identities people hold (figure 5.2) and how the identities you hold intersect with others.

FIGURE 5.2 | **Identities people hold**

Reviewing the personnel policy through an EDI lens is not easy, but is critically important if you want to create an equitable organization. After reviewing the feedback from the EDI consultant and making any changes (Draft 5), review it one more time (Draft 6/Final Draft) before sending it to the board for approval. If possible, don't look at it for a month and then review to give yourself a clearer head when reading it. If you have staff in a union, the union may need to review new policies that would impact staff in the union. Check with your union steward and union contract.

SHARING WITH STAFF

After the board has approved the new or updated policies, it should be shared with staff. In the case of an update of the full personnel policy, a plan should be created to communicate the change to staff and when the change is taking place. Create a memo that details the major (and minor) changes in the new personnel policy and why the changes are happening.

For policies that don't have as much of an impact on staff, still let the staff know the change has taken place. However, no matter what the change, always inform staff why the policy is being adopted and the purpose of the policy. Every time you update the full policy manual, ask staff to read it and sign off that they agree to abide by the personnel policy.

PROCEDURES

While the policy is the guiding principle of the organization, procedures are how those policies play out in the day-to-day operations of the library. Not only are procedures helpful for new and existing staff, but they also provide needed documentation for succession planning, which we will talk about in chapter 9 (Staffing Needs and Succession Planning).. Procedures can take many forms, and a template for library-wide procedures can ensure consistency:

- Procedure name
- Date created/updated
- File path of where the procedure is stored
- Purpose—one to two sentences on the goal of the procedure
- General information—gives a general overview and basic information that staff need to consider before following the steps of the policy
- Procedure—here is the list of steps for staff to complete; depending on the complexity of the procedure, steps may be listed chronologically, by department, or by workflow

When training new staff or handling personnel issues, procedures provide a framework for expectations. Procedure manuals should be stored in a central location for library-wide and departmental procedures. Having a staff intranet or staff drive allows staff access to the procedures they need to effectively do their jobs. If your library does not have the technology for online access, have a current procedure manual binder accessible in each department.

There may be no written procedures for routine library tasks or there may be a manual that is dated. Documenting procedures and creating a manual can be accomplished as staff have the time and become comfortable in their role. Having staff work on day-to-day procedures throughout the year by keeping a list of their common tasks will serve the dual purpose of documenting procedures and ensuring you have up-to-date training materials when a new employee comes on board. When crafting procedures, write them in a way that helps a staff member who has to step in and do the task unexpectedly.

Together, your policies and procedures are the foundation for outlining what your employees can expect from you and what you expect from them and reflect the library's values and vision.

APPLYING YOUR LEARNING: WORKERS' COMPENSATION SCENARIO

Jane was returning from lunch and fell as she entered the building. She limped past the office of the director, who asked if she was okay. Jane mentioned that she had rolled her ankle coming back in the building after lunch. The library director told her to put it on ice and check in with her later.

After reviewing the emergency manual for handling employee injuries, the director went to the door and took pictures of the door threshold (it was a flat threshold leading from a flat tile to flat concrete with no cracks) and noted the time and weather. She called the library's workers' compensation carrier and asked if this could be a WC claim since she was on library property, though clocked out for lunch, and not done during the commission of Jane's work duties. They said yes since Jane was on library property, and even though she didn't injure herself during work, she was returning for work after lunch. They recommended filing a claim just to be safe.

The library director called Jane into the office and asked how her ankle was. Jane said it was very painful and really swollen and she had an appointment to see her doctor after her shift. The director explained that she was going to file a claim with WC and to have the doctor's office bill as a WC claim.

After Jane went to the doctor she discovered she had a serious injury and would require surgery. When she returned from her FMLA leave, her doctor required her to return to work with accommodations because the surgery did not remedy her injury. The library director started the ADA interactive process with Jane in an effort to bring her back to work safely. Jane returned to work utilizing the ADA accommodations worked out with the library director through the ADA interactive process.

QUESTIONS

1. What is the primary issue in this scenario?
2. Who are the players involved?
3. What went well in how this was handled?
4. What should have been handled differently? Why?
5. What laws might come into play on this topic?
6. How would you have approached handling this scenario?

KEY TAKEAWAYS

Personnel policies are guidelines and rules approved by the board that lay out the expectations for staff. Procedures are the instructions for how to accomplish tasks and carry out the policies.

Ensure your policies are up to date by doing a comprehensive review every three to five years with a review by an attorney and EDI consultant as part of the process.

Procedures should be written for certain policies, and additional procedures based on the core tasks should be written and kept up to date.

REFLECTION QUESTIONS FOR CHAPTER 5

- Does your library have an up-to-date personnel policy?
- What policies are missing or need to be updated?
- Have you looked at your personnel policies through an EDI lens?
- Do you, your staff, and your board of trustees evaluate library personnel policies on a regular basis?
- What procedures do you have in place? Are they written down and accessible to staff? How and when are they updated?

ADDITIONAL RESOURCES

CliffsNotes. "HR Management: Laws and Regulations." www.cliffsnotes.com/study-guides/principles-of-management/staffing-and-human-resource-management/hr-management-laws-and-regulations.

Joubert, Shayna. "Laws and Regulations Every HR Professional Should Know." Northeastern blog, September 30, 2020. www.northeastern.edu/graduate/blog/hr-laws-to-know.

Society for Human Resources Management. "Federal Statutes, Regulations and Guidance." www.shrm.org/resourcesandtools/legal-and-compliance/employment-law/pages/federal-statutes-regulations-and-guidance.aspx.

NOTE

1. The Public Library Director's Toolkit, www.librarydirectorstoolkit.com.

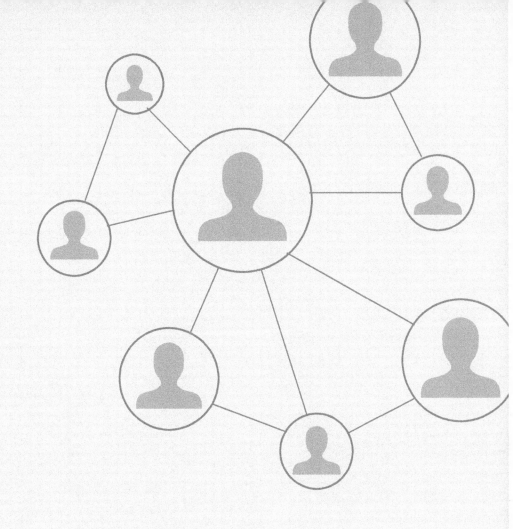

PART II
HR TOOLBOX
Develop and Retain

CHAPTER 6

Feedback and Evaluation

After reading this chapter you will know the following:

+ How to set up communication processes with staff
+ How to provide effective feedback to staff
+ How to perform annual evaluations and why they are necessary
+ How to develop SMART goals for individual staff members

|||||||||||||||||||||||||||||||||||||||||||||||||||||||||||||||||||||||||||||||||||||||||||||||||||||||||||||||||||||||||||||||||||||

O nce a staff member is onboarded, keep them on a track for future success and extend their life cycle within your organization through regular communication, feedback, and evaluation. Communication, feedback, and evaluation form a circle that will allow you to develop and retain strong staff.

COMMUNICATION

Before you can provide feedback to staff, you have to know how to communicate effectively. There are several different ways of looking at communication styles from using a tool like DiSC assessment to understanding the passive vs. assertive behavioral model. While it can be helpful to use formal assessments and tools, you can also discover more about you and your staff's communication styles by talking with staff:

- How do they process information? Are they internal processors and need time to think through things ahead of time? Or are they external processors and want to talk it through in the moment?
- What level of communication do you expect from your staff member in terms of updates, status reports, and so on?
- What level of communication does your employee expect from you as their manager?

- Have your employee think about a manager whom they struggled to communicate effectively with and one whom they communicated really well with. Have them describe what worked and what didn't to help glean insights into their preferred communication methods and styles.

Staff new to the workforce might not be able to answer these questions. In that case, you want to observe and talk through the questions with staff to help uncover the answers. The key is to have a shared language you can use to help understand each other's communication styles. Effective communication ensures that you and your staff can carry out the mission of the library and provide the best library service possible for your community.

COMMUNICATION METHODS

Understanding how people think and process information is helpful, but the method used also matters:

- Written (email, text/Slack/GChat, written reports)
- Verbal (phone, face to face, video conferencing, group meetings)
- Nonverbal (seen in both written and verbal)

Written messages tend to be better for relaying complex information that needs to be referred back to or simple messages that do not require feedback, while verbal communication is better for more immediate or timely communication or for more in-depth discussions. But with either method, consider the nonverbal cues that play a role. Nonverbal communication can be used both intentionally and unintentionally. When considering what method to use, think through what nonverbal message you might be sending alongside your written or verbal message. Knowing the type of message you are relaying and the way people process information will help you deliver the message effectively.

The best way to determine your employee's preferred communication methods is to ask them and then reciprocate with yours. While you may not always be able to communicate using their preferred method, having a sense of how they prefer to communicate will help remove barriers to communication. Lay out clear expectations if you have certain items you want communicated in a certain way like a written monthly report. Provide feedback on what they are communicating to let them know if it is too much, not enough, leaving out key info, or exactly what you are looking for. The clearer you can be on what you are looking for, the easier it will be for your staff to provide you with the information you need.

NAVIGATING COMMUNICATION ROADBLOCKS

If you run into communication roadblocks, share what is working and what isn't. A tool to help discuss this is Start, Stop, Continue (figure 6.1):

FIGURE 6.1 | **Start, stop, and continue**

START	**STOP**	**CONTINUE**
What should we **START** doing to improve/ strengthen our communication?	What should we **STOP** doing that is impeding effective communication?	What should we **CONTINUE** doing because it is working well?

FEEDBACK

When people hear the word *feedback*, many immediately automatically assume that it will be negative. But feedback should be so much more than a corrective action. Feedback should:

- Be ongoing and consistent and woven into the regular meetings and interactions you have with your staff.
- Provide both positive reinforcement of tasks done well and constructive suggestions for helping the employee learn and grow.
- Flow from you to your staff and from your staff to you.

GIVING FEEDBACK

Feedback should happen for every employee, but depending on where the employee is in their career path, the type of feedback may change. For new employees, you might need to give more detailed feedback to help them learn. For more established employees, you want to provide feedback in a way that allows them to draw on their past skills and experience to grow.

When giving feedback, make sure you are clear on what you are telling them and the reasons for the feedback. If you tend to do tasks a certain way and your employee does them a different way, but both result in the task being accomplished correctly in a timely manner, then you don't need to provide feedback on how the task was done. Your goal in providing feedback is to help your employee learn and grow in their position, not to micromanage how their work is accomplished.

Providing feedback doesn't have to be complicated or take long. There are some steps to take to ensure feedback will be most helpful to your employee:

- Establish trust
- Be specific
- Focus on the actions, not the person
- Provide feedback in a timely manner
- Use clear language

We will talk in more detail about feedback as it relates to discipline in chapter 11 (Discipline and Termination). If your library has a union, there might be specific language in the contract that provides structure around how to give feedback to staff.

Establish Trust

Establishing trust doesn't happen overnight. But you can establish trust with staff over time by being consistent in providing feedback, being honest about your own failings and opportunities for growth, and displaying empathy.

> BAD: I never made mistakes like this when I was in your position.
> BETTER: When I was a new librarian, I hadn't been trained on how to properly weed and ended up heavily weeding our fairy tale collection right before the third-graders came in for a project. I can imagine how you are feeling right now. Let's talk about helping you learn more about weeding.

Be Specific

For feedback to be useful, it needs to be specific. Make sure to reference the work that was done and why it was great or not up to par.

> BAD: Good job on the presentation today.
> BETTER: Your presentation today was very interactive and ensured that all the participants were actively engaged in the online training. Good job on crafting such an engaging presentation.

Focus on the Actions, Not the Person

When giving feedback, never focus on the person. It is not about who they are, but about what they are doing. What actions have they taken and what impact do their actions have on others in the organization?

> BAD: You are always late to work and don't value other people's time.
>
> BETTER: When you consistently arrive late to work, others need to cover your desk shift. This prevents them from working on other tasks and has a negative impact on the department.

Provide Feedback in a Timely Manner

Positive feedback can be given in the moment. But you can also wait and bring it up at your next one-on-one meeting. You can use the Start, Stop, Continue method discussed above if you struggle with giving feedback.

Managers often struggle to give constructive feedback. This is more important to do in a timely manner so that the staff member can remember what occurred and think about how they could have acted differently.

> BAD: Last month I noticed you being curt with someone who needed help with technology. That needs to stop.
>
> BETTER: Earlier today, I noticed that you were losing patience while helping Mr. Smith use one of our databases. This is the third time in the past month that I have observed similar interactions. As we have discussed previously, we expect staff to work patiently with patrons on technology issues.

Use Clear Language

When providing feedback, make sure you use clear and direct language. Don't try to imply what actions you want people to take. Don't use the "sandwich" method of giving feedback by starting and ending with a compliment when giving constructive feedback. Being direct and clear may be less comfortable for you, but is more beneficial for the staff member.

> BAD: You are bad at customer service.
>
> BETTER: Moving forward, I need you to be polite and respectful to every patron who walks into the department. That means making eye contact, smiling, or saying hello as people approach the desk.

The more consistent you are about feedback frequency, and the more you provide specific, meaningful positive feedback, the more your team learns that feedback is just another tool you use to help them succeed.

PROVIDING FEEDBACK TO MARGINALIZED EMPLOYEES

Multiple studies show that BIPOC staff receive less feedback, which makes it harder for them to learn and gain opportunities for more responsibility.[1] Just like in hiring, managers need to avoid affinity bias by only giving feedback to employees who remind them of themselves. Instead, they need to regularly offer feedback to everyone.

When providing feedback to staff, make sure you are not offering feedback simply to mold them into your idea of an ideal employee. Focus on strengthening their unique skills and abilities and give them space to share the challenges and microaggressions they face in the workplace.

Create a safe space for them and acknowledge what they are experiencing, without taking over the conversation and making the conversation about you or your feelings. Make a commitment to yourself to keep learning and growing so you can better support your marginalized staff.

RECEIVING FEEDBACK

Receiving feedback from others in your organization can be incredibly beneficial. Feedback should be asked for but never demanded. Here are some steps to take to ensure you are receiving the feedback in a way that will allow you to grow as a leader:

- Establish trust
- Listen, then listen harder
- Ask follow-up questions to better understand the feedback
- Take time to process the feedback
- Determine if any action is needed
- Acknowledge the feedback and thank the giver

Establish Trust

Just as in giving feedback, receiving feedback requires a high level of trust. If you are receiving the feedback from someone subordinate to you, that requires trust on their part to share this with you. How you respond to the feedback will determine whether you ever receive any feedback in the future. Tone matters in establishing trust, so if you don't think you can respond in a helpful manner in the moment, thank the staff member for sharing the feedback and tell them you would like to follow up with more questions later that day or tomorrow.

> BAD: What do you mean you don't think I'm listening to staff's concerns about the new procedure?
> BETTER: Thank you for sharing your concerns. I am sorry to hear that you feel your concerns are not being addressed.

Listen, Then Listen Harder

When someone is sharing feedback with you, it is time for you to listen. Don't try to respond immediately. Let the words sink in. Refrain from speaking until they are completely finished speaking.

FROM THE DIRECTOR'S CORNER—KATE'S STORY

There are three things you need to know about me:

- I like to talk.
- I tend to talk a lot.
- I am an eldest child.

I became a manager at nineteen and have been managing for twenty-two years now. I read books on management and followed all the rules. As an eldest child, I believed that I knew what was best in just about every scenario and told anyone who came to me for help exactly what to do. My bosses told me I was doing a good job, and I was confident in my abilities.

Once I became a director, I figured this trend would continue with my board. But that didn't happen. One board president said, "If you are doing something wrong, we'll tell you."

So, I turned to the staff and asked for feedback. And staff had a lot of things they felt I could be doing better. I was floored. I had always been told how good I was at managing.

But I hadn't been good at listening. At first it was hard to hear the feedback. Didn't they know how hard I worked? How much I cared? When I stopped talking and started listening more, I realized that they were giving me the keys to be a better manager.

I still struggle with not dominating every conversation and still love to talk a lot, but I have learned that if I listen, my staff will help me continue to grow into a better leader.

MORAL: In order to grow, you need to listen.

Ask Follow-up Questions to Better Understand the Feedback

When they are done sharing their feedback, ask clarifying questions to better understand the feedback they are giving you.

> BAD: So, you're saying that even though I talked about this at the department meeting and asked staff if they had questions, you are only now telling me you have concerns about the new procedures?
>
> BETTER: What I'm hearing you say is that you felt the process to roll out this new procedure was rushed and that there wasn't enough time to review the procedures and give feedback. You also didn't see a way to offer your feedback and now are feeling stressed about this new procedure. Is that accurate?

Take Time to Process the Feedback

As managers, we often feel that we need to respond immediately. And while this is true when someone is bleeding on the floor, when it comes to feedback, you may not respond well in the moment and need time to think through what was said. Tell the person giving you the feedback that you need a few minutes, a few hours, or a day. (Conversely, if a staff member asks for the same when you are giving them feedback, give them the same courtesy.) Set a concrete date for when you will respond to the employee. If you are feeling uncomfortable with some aspect of the feedback, lean in and get to the root of why you might be feeling that way and what may have triggered that reaction.

> BAD: You're wrong. I actually gave staff multiple opportunities to provide feedback.
>
> BETTER: Thank you for sharing your concerns. I'd like to think about what you have just shared and talk about this again this afternoon.

Determine if Any Action Is Needed

There is an assumption that you must act on all feedback. You do need to acknowledge it, but you don't have to agree with what the person is saying. The feedback they are giving you is their perception of what is happening. They might not have all the information or may be interpreting the information differently than you.

That doesn't mean you should discount all the feedback. Ask questions to understand where the person is coming from and determine if there is anything you can learn from this feedback, even if what you learn is not what the person giving the feedback thinks you need to learn. Keep in mind that we all have blind spots, which means we need to work hard to ensure we are not influenced by our own thoughts when receiving feedback.

Regardless of whether you take specific actions on the feedback, all feedback can be helpful because it gives you greater insight into how that person is thinking and perceiving their work environment. It can clue you in to other issues that might pop up or let you know that the staff member is out of alignment with the organization.

ACKNOWLEDGE THE FEEDBACK WITH A THANKS

Even if you disagree with the feedback, acknowledge the trust it took to share this information. Thank them for sharing their thoughts. How you treat the person giving the feedback will be relayed to others and determine whether you get feedback in the future.

EVALUATION

In addition to providing ongoing feedback, at least once a year there should be a formal or informal evaluation process for each staff member. This may occur on the anniversary date or at the end of the fiscal year. Some libraries might have a very formal process with scoring systems used to determine salary increases while other libraries have a more informal process to talk about what was accomplished in the previous year. Whether formal or informal, an annual process should happen for every employee to help reflect on the year that just passed and talk about goals for the coming year.

FORMAL PROCESS

If your evaluation process is tied into compensation, your evaluation forms need to be tied to clear standards that are equitably applied based on job duties.

While you can create these yourself, working with an HR consultant can ensure that you do not have any bias baked into your rubrics.

Typically, a formal evaluation form will have a scoring rubric based on key job functions from the job description for each job. There will be clearly defined metrics that are used for scoring that both staff and managers understand. The evaluation forms should reflect what has occurred throughout the year. There should not be any surprises for staff. Instead, this should reflect the many talks the managers have had with their staff throughout the past year.

In addition to having the formal evaluation form, have each staff member fill out a self-evaluation to reflect on what they have accomplished in the year and identify areas for further learning and development. Evaluations should be reviewed to ensure that they are consistent. Are managers scoring similar positions the same across departments? Are there clear examples of when someone is exceeding expectations, or is the manager just giving everyone top scores because they like their staff? Performance reviews can invite a lot of bias, and having an impartial process is critical.

Once the self-evaluations and evaluations are completed and reviewed, managers will meet one-on-one with each staff member to review them. At this time, if the evaluations are tied to compensation, salary increases should be shared with staff and they should be notified of how these are determined. When doing a more formal process, make sure you are sharing with staff what the process is and how it was developed.

INFORMAL PROCESS

You can also adopt a more informal process. You should still have the staff member complete a self-evaluation to reflect on the previous year, but then you can have a shorter narrative form for managers to complete that summarizes what was accomplished and the areas of focus for the coming year. Just as with the formal evaluation process, there should never be a surprise in what is written.

Once completed, each manager should meet one-on-one with each of their direct reports. Have a list of questions to cover that you share ahead of time with staff, such as:

- What are you most proud of accomplishing in the past year?
- What was a challenge you faced in the past year and how did you handle it? What did you learn from this experience?
- What is one thing you have learned in the past year? How have you used what you learned in your role?

- What can I do to better support you in your role?
- What is one new thing you would like to learn next year?

SETTING GOALS

During this annual process, employees should be given the opportunity to reflect on their successes and failures of the previous year, and the manager should do the same. Then, the manager and employee should meet to reflect on the past year together and set goals for the coming year.

When setting up goals, make sure they are SMART (figure 6.2).

There are many arguments for and against formal and informal evaluation processes, but whichever route you take, stopping to reflect on previous performance and taking the time to look ahead at what you want to accomplish is important to your overall organization and to individual employee success and engagement. Having a process in place guarantees that this critical step is not overlooked.

FIGURE 6.2 | **SMART Goals**

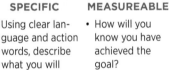

SPECIFIC	MEASUREABLE	ACHIEVABLE	RELEVANT	TIME-BOUND
• Using clear language and action words, describe what you will accomplish.	• How will you know you have achieved the goal? • What are you basing success on?	• Is it something that is possible to accomplish? • Do you have the bandwidth to accomplish this?	• Does this fit in with my role in the library? • Is this something the library needs done?	• When will this be accomplished?

APPLYING YOUR LEARNING: PRONOUN BADGE FAILURE

The Washington Public Library had developed a set of core values: innovation, excellence, and inclusion. As part of this work, the Reference manager asked staff for suggestions on what they could do to make the department more inclusive. A staff member suggested putting employees' pronouns on everyone's name tag. The manager made staff fill out a form with their pronouns and then ordered new name tags.

Some staff were happy to have their pronouns listed on the name tags while others complained about being forced to have it on their name tag. Some didn't really understand why the library had done this or know what to say if a patron asked a question.

Marty had been watching the library's inclusion work closely. They (Marty) were nonbinary and used they/them pronouns. But they had not shared their pronouns at work and felt uncomfortable about the way the name tags were rolled out. Marty overheard two coworkers making discriminatory comments about pronouns. The manager clearly overheard them, but didn't say anything and turned and walked away. The manager did not bring up what was overheard in one-on-ones or in the staff member's annual evaluation. Marty left the library soon after, not feeling psychologically or emotionally safe.

QUESTIONS

1. What is the primary issue in this scenario?
2. Who are the players involved?
3. What went well in how this was handled?
4. What should have been handled differently? Why?
5. What laws might come into play on this topic?
6. How would you have approached handling this scenario?

KEY TAKEAWAYS

Feedback revolves around being able to communicate effectively verbally, nonverbally, and in writing. Giving consistent feedback to staff is essential and easier if you follow these steps:

- Establish trust
- Be specific
- Focus on the actions, not the person
- Provide feedback in a timely manner
- Use clear language

Receiving feedback is a skill all managers should cultivate. The steps to receive feedback with a growth mindset are:

- Establish trust
- Listen, then listen harder
- Ask follow-up questions to better understand
- Take time to process the feedback
- Determine if any action is necessary

In addition to feedback, libraries should do either formal or informal annual evaluations and have staff set SMART goals for the following year.

REFLECTION QUESTIONS FOR CHAPTER 6

- How do I currently provide feedback to my direct reports?
- What can I do to improve how I give feedback?
- What steps can I take to make staff more comfortable with giving me feedback?
- What does our evaluation process look like? How does it tie into our job descriptions, training requirements, and other feedback?

ADDITIONAL RESOURCES

Harvard Business Review. *HBR Guide to Delivering Effective Feedback*. Boston: Harvard Business Review Press, 2016.

Society for Human Resources Management. "HR Forms & Checklists." www.shrm.org/resourcesandtools/tools-and-samples/hr-forms/pages/default.aspx.

Stone, Douglas. *Thanks for the Feedback: The Science and Art of Receiving Feedback Well*. New York: Viking, 2014.

NOTE

1. Zuhairah Washington and Laura Morgan Roberts, "Women of Color Get Less Support at Work. Here's How Managers Can Change That," *Harvard Business Review*, March 4, 2019, https://hbr.org/2019/03/women-of-color-get-less-support-at-work-heres-how-managers-can-change-that.

CHAPTER 7

Continual Training and Career Development

After reading this chapter you will know the following:

+ How to construct a training framework for employees
+ What types of internal training to offer staff
+ Why continual training is critical to your library's success
+ How to provide individual growth opportunities for staff

||||||||||||||||||||||||||||||||||||||||||||||||||||||||||||||||||||||||||||||||||||||||||||||||||||||||||||||||||||||||||||||||||||

Providing feedback is a critical component to managing an employee, but employees need to learn in other ways as well. Managers need to provide staff with opportunities for continual training and growth, which will also help in extending the life cycle of an employee in the organization. Libraries as institutions of lifelong learning need to help staff be lifelong learners as well. In order to serve their community, staff must engage in ongoing training and development to keep their skills up to date. Continual training is also important to provide opportunities for staff that want to grow in the library profession. Depending on your state, there may be a certain number of CE hours staff are required to complete for certification or other requirements.

CONTINUAL TRAINING

Continual training does not mean that staff are training constantly. Libraries should have a training plan in place for key training and a budget that allows staff at all levels to engage in learning throughout their employment. Depending on your library size and budget, you will need to consider how much internal and external training is possible.

TRAINING FRAMEWORK

We often talk about the importance of training, but to be effective, you need to build a training framework. Managers and staff should take steps to help the learning stick so staff apply what is learned to their work.

Training Preparation

Before someone goes to a training, they should reflect on why they are attending and what they hope to learn. Have a training request form that asks staff why they want to go and what they hope to learn.

In the case of internal training, have the presenter outline the goals and objectives of the training. Giving staff a clear goal on why they are taking the training will help them apply it to their position.

Training Follow-up

After the training is completed, staff should reflect on what they learned. If the training was hands-on, check in with staff to see if they have follow-up questions and encourage them to take time to play with whatever they learned. If they attended a training on something you or other staff don't know, have them talk about what they learned with a larger group. Teaching someone else reinforces the training for the trainer.

When a training is more about the future of libraries or other big picture topics, have a discussion with the staff member afterward to help them form opinions on what they value and where they see their position/department/library in terms of what was presented.

The level of the training will dictate how much reflection is needed. A one-hour training might merit a one- or two-sentence reflection while a five-day conference might result in a written summary, a one-on-one discussion, and a department discussion.

Additional Follow-up

Not every training will require a second follow-up but, in some instances, you may want to check in again to see how employees apply the learning further out. A good time to do this is during the annual evaluation process.

The goal of the training framework is to give staff space to reflect and provide time for real growth. Now that you know how to reinforce training, what training should staff attend?

INTERNAL TRAINING

All libraries should offer some sort of internal training for staff on:

- Library and department procedures
- Emergency procedures
- Ongoing training in leadership, technology, collection development, and customer service

Develop a schedule and a list of training that you will provide for staff. There are many different methods to offer internal training to staff:

- General library-wide staff in-service day training
- Departmental training
- Specialized training on new products and services
- Recorded trainings
- Informal in-the-moment training

You will also need to adopt a plan for new staff who will need to be trained on all of this as well.

FROM THE DIRECTOR'S CORNER—KATE'S STORY

As a director, I wanted to ensure all of the service desks were offering consistently excellent service, so I devised a series of training to lay out our library's service expectations and train staff. We did training sessions once a month for six months, and started getting more positive patron comments soon after. I patted myself on the back and considered this task complete.

Over time, patron complaints about service started increasing again. I had never done any follow-up training and had not had any of the new staff go through the training sessions. I had improved service for a bit, but hadn't made it a key focus by offering follow-up training and training for new staff.

MORAL: To keep important skills front of mind, make sure to offer regular training for new and existing staff.

Library and Department Procedures

In order to offer training on basic library and department procedures, you need to have written procedures on the work done throughout the library. As your library makes changes, procedures will be updated and you will need to offer updated training to staff. This training can happen either formally or informally depending on the level of change. A small update to your integrated library system (ILS) may only require an email, while a migration to a new ILS would require more formal training.

Emergency Procedures

Every library should have written emergency procedures on what to do in the case of different emergencies such as a fire alarm, active threat, or power outage. You need to regularly review the procedures with staff and do practice drills. Working with your local police and fire departments can ensure that first responders know what training is offered and give staff the opportunity to ask questions.

In addition to regular emergency training for staff, you also need to train managers and persons in charge (PICs). These trainings will cover what to do when they are in charge and an emergency happens.

Often emergency training is done on an annual basis and is more a lecture than hands-on. Doing physical drills and then talking through what worked and what didn't will allow you to create emergency procedures that are effective and give staff a chance to practice how they would react in different scenarios.

Ongoing Training

Staff in libraries need to be well versed on a variety of different topics. Ongoing training in the areas of leadership, technology, collection management, and customer service is helpful to keep staff skills up to date.

Develop a list of the core skills staff need to have and what refreshers are needed to keep up with changes in the field. A variety of great resources for training are available, so you don't necessarily need to do all the training internally, but you will need to consider your library's core values when thinking through what training to offer. If one of the core values is inclusion and you want to provide training on collection management, make sure the training offered reflects that value and not only discusses techniques like using the CREW method's MUSTIE criteria but also encompasses diversity audits and buying books written by diverse authors.

Training Methods

Based on what you are going to be training staff on, there are several ways to offer training:

- General library staff training
- Departmental training
- Specialized training on new products and services
- Recorded trainings
- Informal in-the-moment training

Regular staff training is critical to keep staff connected and informed. Many libraries have one or two days a year they close for a full day and bring in staff to do training. Others choose to open late one day a month and do smaller bursts of training. Choose whichever works best for your library and community. Be sure you have time dedicated to staff training that provides staff a chance to connect with each other, build stronger relationships, and train everyone on specific procedures.

When you are rolling out a new product, service, or procedure, construct a training plan as part of the rollout and give staff a chance to learn formally and informally by playing with the product before it gets rolled out. If your staff is larger or works very different schedules, consider offering recorded training that staff can watch.

For training to be continual, be on the lookout for ways to train staff in the moment and encourage others to help each other learn new things. If you see someone struggling with searching for an item in the catalog, show them the tricks you have learned. If you need help constructing a pivot table, ask someone who you know is good at Excel for help. By encouraging ongoing learning, staff will be more flexible with change and embrace learning as part of your library's culture.

EXTERNAL TRAINING

Along with in-house training, staff should be given opportunities to learn outside the library. Your library's staff size and budget will determine what external training you can send staff to. The library field has a plethora of training at the local, state, and national level that staff can take. These trainings typically fall into three categories:

- Continuing education workshops
- Online learning
- Conferences

When considering what external training to offer staff, don't just rely on library training. Look for training from specialists who can help with topics that reach beyond libraries:

- Equity, diversity, and inclusion
- HR
- Building maintenance
- Customer service
- Graphic design and marketing
- Technology and innovation
- Project management
- Data analysis

While our field has a wealth of knowledge, we should not only look to other libraries to learn, but seek out training from outside the library world to ensure we are remaining relevant and up to date on national and global trends.

Continuing Education (CE) Workshops

CE workshops are offered at all levels in the library world. These can be in person or online. When considering what you can send staff to, remember that if they are traveling to an in-person workshop, you will need to reimburse them for their time spent driving to and from as well as mileage. Look at what types of CE offerings you have at the local, state, and national level. Many American Library Association divisions and state library associations offer a wide variety of in-person and online training to help staff learn and grow.

Online Learning

Offering staff access to online learning is a way to provide training for a library on a tight budget. ALA offers a variety of online learning opportunities, as does Web Junction. Look at what databases you offer to patrons and see if there are training opportunities for staff as well.

Conferences

Conferences are usually the most expensive training offering. These events can be overwhelming for a first-time conference-goer, but they offer a wide array of ways to learn and network. Conferences offer sessions to attend as well as exhibit halls, round tables, and other opportunities to connect with colleagues around the state or country. When considering who to send to out-of-state conferences, many libraries need to prioritize based on budgetary constraints. Because of the cost per person to send, house, feed, and pay for conference attendance, building a training framework is even more important. If your library is able to send multiple people to a conference, meet with everyone beforehand to discuss what you are planning to attend, plan for connecting during the conference, and then schedule a time to talk afterward about what you learned.

There is a rich array of internal and external training opportunities for staff. By utilizing the training framework, you will help staff not only attend meaningful training, but be able to apply what they learn to their work.

CAREER DEVELOPMENT

Regular training for staff at all levels is key to building a strong workforce, but what about staff that want to grow in their current position or into a different position? Helping staff develop leads to a stronger profession and better staff engagement. There are a number of different ways to help staff grow, but first you need to learn what staff want for their future. During the annual evaluation or at a one-on-one meeting, provided you have established a trusting relationship with your employee and they have indicated a desire for career advancement, ask:

- How would you like to use your skills in the future?
- What knowledge and skills do you need to get to the next stage of your career? (They might not know the answer to this, which can lead to a discussion with you as their manager.)
- How can I support you in your development?

Remember, not everyone wants to move up the organizational hierarchy, and that's okay. You can still help staff who want to grow their skills, whether it is becoming the best they can be in their chosen position or to move to a higher-level position. Once you have a sense of where staff are at and what support they might need, there are a number of different ways to help staff that can be used individually or together:

- Professional development plan
- Mentoring
- Coaching
- Project-based development

PROFESSIONAL DEVELOPMENT PLAN (PDP)

A professional development plan is like a performance improvement plan, except that you focus on growing skills that staff need to become an expert in their job or to grow into another position rather than on correcting performance issues. In a union environment, look at the contract to determine if you have the flexibility to allow staff to participate in this type of learning.

Start by working with the staff member to determine what skills and knowledge they need to acquire. If they are not sure, look at a job description for the position they hope to get someday or look at someone who is a rock star in that particular role. List what knowledge and skills they need to obtain to be successful in that role.

Once you have the topics nailed down, create specific goals on what needs to be learned based on what the staff member already knows. Keeping in mind that this is supplemental to the regular work they have on their plate, develop a training timeline and schedule to meet up to discuss how it is going. You can either choose to do a comprehensive PDP that covers all the topics and spans a longer time frame, or you can focus on one or two topics and span a couple months. Whatever route you go, make sure you are checking in with the staff member and discussing what they are learning. A sample PDP is available on our website.

MENTORING

A mentor can be a very formal role with specific guidelines and objectives, or it can be more informal and exist either within your organization or with people outside the organization. Cambridge University defines mentoring as "the act or process of helping and giving advice to a younger or less experienced person, especially in a job or at school."[1] Sometimes the word *mentor* is not even used, but the unofficial mentor still serves the following functions:

- Provides guidance to an employee seeking to grow into a different position.
- Shares their experiences, insights, and feedback with the employee to help them grow.
- Reviews their own career path.
- Highlights mistakes and failures they experienced and what they learned from them.
- Serves as a supporter and offers encouragement to the mentee.

Mentoring can be paired with a PDP or operate on its own.

Depending on the type of mentoring relationship, mentor and mentee may meet weekly, monthly, quarterly, or yearly. The frequency and structure of the meetings should be discussed at the outset so both parties have a clear view of what is being offered and expected.

COACHING

Unlike mentoring, coaching is less about imparting knowledge than about helping the employee think through how they would handle different situations and where they want to go. Coaching can be offered by a manager, peer, or someone outside the organization. A coach's goal is to keep the employee accountable and on track by listening and asking questions. There are numerous resources for coaching, some of which are listed at the end of this chapter, but here are some tips when coaching an employee:

- Listen 80–90 percent; talk 10–20 percent.
- Ask open-ended questions like "What would success look like for this situation?"
- Avoid starting questions with *Why*, such as "Why did you handle it that way?"
- Ask follow-up questions like "Tell me more about that."
- Probe for deeper reflection with questions like "Help me understand" or "Tell me more about why you feel this way."

Some sample coaching questions you can use with employees include:

- What is working well right now?
- What is your goal/desired outcome in this situation?
- What else do you need to consider?
- What might another way of looking at this situation be?
- What can you learn from this situation?
- What do you need from me right now?

Coaching tends to be focused on helping the employee over a shorter period of time and focuses on one or two specific areas.

PROJECT-BASED DEVELOPMENT

You can also offer staff learning opportunities on a case-by-case basis. By giving staff at all levels opportunities to learn new skills, you will create a stronger organization and keep staff engaged. One way to do this is to offer staff the chance to chair internal work groups and committees and encourage staff to get involved outside the library in the community, state, and national organizations like ALA.

Internally, consider giving a staff member who has the desire to become a manager the opportunity to be the chair for a project. Giving them the ability to chair a larger group and project will teach them how to effectively run meetings or manage a project. Externally, encourage staff to become involved in local service groups like Lions, Rotary, or Kiwanis or other community organizations like the historical society or chamber of commerce. At the state or national levels, there are many opportunities to become involved within the library profession.

In order to be ready to meet the challenges of the future, staff must engage in ongoing training and development to ensure they are ready to make those changes. Whether internal or external, training should be woven into the culture of your library.

APPLYING YOUR LEARNING: I DON'T NEED ANYTHING OTHER THAN MY DEGREE

Suzy graduated with her master's in library science, and worked her way up from interlibrary loan clerk to library director of a medium-size library. When attending regional library director meetings, the other library directors would often discuss the continuing education training they had attended.

Suzy never attended the discussed training sessions. Her reply was always, "I went to library school and got my master's degree. I don't need additional training."

Two years later, Suzy was terminated. The board discovered that Suzy had not been complying with the new minimum wage laws. When they brought in an interim director, they found many policies in direct violation of laws, and necessary filings and documentation had not been saved. The library was a complete mess and it would take some time to get it back in order.

QUESTIONS

1. What is the primary issue in this scenario?
2. Who are the players involved?
3. What went well in how this was handled?
4. What should have been handled differently? Why?
5. What laws might come into play on this topic?
6. How would you have approached handling this scenario?

KEY TAKEAWAYS

Libraries should give staff opportunities to learn and grow in their roles while also providing library-wide training on key topics for staff. In order to get the most out of training, follow the training framework with staff:

- Before they go, have staff reflect on what they hope to learn.
- After training, follow up with staff to talk about key takeaways and applying what they learned.
- Further down the road, circle back with staff to see how applying the various training they have attended is going.

Helping staff grow in their roles and the profession can be done using different tools:

- Professional development plan
- Mentoring
- Coaching
- Project-based development

Libraries as institutions of lifelong learning must also put together a plan to help their staff be lifelong learners as well.

REFLECTION QUESTIONS FOR CHAPTER 7

- How do you engage with staff when they go to a training workshop to ensure they are reflecting on what they learn and applying it to their work?
- What internal training do you currently offer staff on core topics?
- What outside training do you offer staff to help them learn and connect with colleagues?
- What opportunities have you given staff from marginalized populations to develop their careers?

ADDITIONAL RESOURCES

Pratchett, Terry. *Practical Tips for Developing Your Staff.* London: Facet, 2016.

Reed, Lori. *Workplace Learning & Leadership: A Handbook for Library and Nonprofit Trainers.* Chicago: ALA Editions, 2011.

Society for Human Resources Management. "Developing Employees by SHRM."
    SHRM Toolkits. www.shrm.org/resourcesandtools/tools-and-samples/
    toolkits/pages/developingemployees.aspx.
Stanier, Michael Bungay. *The Coaching Habit*. Vancouver, Page Two, 2016.

NOTE

1. *Cambridge Dictionary*, s.v. "Mentoring," https://dictionary.cambridge.org/us/
dictionary/english/mentoring.

CHAPTER 8

Employee Engagement and Strengthening Morale

After reading this chapter you will know the following:

+ Why leadership plays a key role in employee engagement and strengthening morale
+ How to assess morale and engagement and act on the results
+ What tips and strategies exist to strengthen morale

|||||||||||||||||||||||||||||||||||||||||||||||||||||||||||||||||||||||||||||||||||||||||||||||||||||||||||||||||||||||||||||||||||||||||||||

The morale of individual staff members ties in directly with how engaged employees are in the organization. While staff morale focuses on the employee's individual feelings, attitudes, general outlook, and satisfaction level, employee engagement describes the commitment individual employees feel to the mission, vision, and values of the library. Each correlates to the other, and when one dips so too does the other, leading to decreased productivity and service. Keeping a staff member engaged will not only improve employee retention but will mean better service for your community and improved morale. Both require strong communication within your organization.

YOUR ROLE AS A LEADER

As a leader, staff morale and employee engagement start with you.

In order to engage employees, your library needs to have a clear mission, dynamic vision, and defined values. Employees need to know what they are signing up for when they come to your organization and what they can expect in the work environment. Once you have defined who you are as an organization, your job as leader means putting those words into practice.

If your library says it values innovation, but then repeatedly calls people to task for trying new programs or failing with a new venture, then you are not matching your words with your behavior, and employees will disengage.

You need to be engaged as well. If you as the leader don't care about the mission of the library, then why should your staff? You as a leader need to not only be clear on your organization's mission, vision, and values, but know your own values. If you have never taken the time to develop your list of core values, here are some questions you can ask yourself to help think about what values are important to you:

- Think about the moments you are most proud of. What made you proud and what values were at play?
- Conversely, think about the moments that you were least proud of. Why did you feel that way? What values were at play?
- Who is important in your life? Why? How would you define their core values?
- What is your definition of success?
- What are the issues/topics/items that you will not budge on?
- When do you feel really "on" and when do you feel "off"? What separates the two?

Once you have defined your core values you will be able to see how they align with the library's mission, vision, and values. These core values are what guide your actions, whether you have taken the time to define them or not. In defining your core values, make sure that you are also creating space for the additional values that staff may have that motivate them. Those are another important piece in creating an inclusive culture in your library.

As a library director, you are the spokesperson for the library in the community, but you are also the spokesperson for the library with staff. Staff can tell if you are not authentic in your words and actions.

The culture of an organization is shaped by many in the organization, but requires the leader's buy-in and actions to cement it into place. A leader with strong core values who embodies their values and the values of the library in their words and actions will send positive ripple effects throughout the entire staff.

ASSESS THE ENVIRONMENT

Now that you as a leader are clear on your role, how do you go about engaging staff? You want them to be engaged with the purpose of the library but first you need to be interested in who they are and focus on creating a welcoming environment. Part of employee engagement is recognizing that people hold many different identities and will have additional values they bring with them. When looking for ways to engage staff, leaders need to think about how they can be welcoming and inclusive for the different identities and values their staff hold. Offer opportunities for staff to build relationships with each other that allows them to connect through the interests they hold like sports teams, TV shows, music, and so on. This is a low threat investment in fostering a more connected organization. You should always be moving your organization toward an environment where everyone feels that they can be authentic.

In order to assess where your organization is at, the first step is to gather information by looking at your environment:

- Is your building accessible to staff who have disabilities?
- What do you do to support staff who are from marginalized or often underrepresented groups such as Black, Indigenous, People of Color, LGBTQ+, English language learners, or workers with disabilities?
- How do you show staff that you welcome and value the unique skills they bring to the library?
- What steps has the library taken to ensure staff feel psychologically and emotionally safe at work?
- How do you recognize staff for their achievements?
- How do you facilitate staff's success and help them learn from failures?
- Why do they work at your library and what do they like most (and least) about the organization?

These are hard questions, and because we all have unconscious biases, assessing your library is best done with a consultant who can guide you through an assessment.

Surveying staff is one way to find out where morale is at and how engaged they are. Surveying the staff and then acting on the findings helps the organization know how satisfied staff are in their role or in the organization. It helps determine what additional opportunities or training they are looking for, and if there are areas of concern that need to be addressed. Being proactive in addressing as many concerns as you can will ensure staff morale stays high and employees stay engaged.

FROM THE DIRECTOR'S CORNER—KATE'S STORY

When I was a newish director, I wanted to implement technology competencies so that staff would have core technology skill requirements based on their position. We evaluated staff to see which areas we needed to do training in to get people up to the basic level of technology understanding for their position. I then devised what I thought was a brilliant idea to roll out the training. We would have a gameboard with all the staff's names, and each time they completed a training they would get a sticker to move through the gameboard. Eventually one person would win the game and get a prize.

I am very motivated by competition, but my staff was not. They hated this idea of gamifying the training and were horrified at the thought of having how many training sessions they had completed up for all to see. I listened to staff and instead of having the game board, we set personal goals for each staff member. If they completed their goals, they would get paid time off or be entered into a drawing for a gift card at the end of the training. Staff loved it and suddenly everyone on staff was completing training like crazy.

MORAL: Thinking you have a good idea doesn't make it so. Listen to staff to find out what they want.

As managers, we often think we know our staff and how they feel about the library, but you should go directly to the source. Ask your staff either in small groups, individually, or in a survey what they need to feel engaged and what will cause them to disengage. Once you have gathered the information and analyzed the results based on identity and their role within the organization, you will discover how happy and engaged your staff actually are and what needs to be done to increase their satisfaction and engagement. Make sure to have a way for staff to provide ongoing ideas and suggestions that can strengthen morale and engagement and a plan for how to take those ideas and turn them into actions. This work is a continuous loop and you should regularly revisit how staff are feeling to keep morale and engagement high.

ACTING ON YOUR FINDINGS

There is no one true way to keep morale high and staff engaged, but by listening to staff and finding out what they need to feel engaged in the organization, you will be able to create a plan for your library. You can create a formal plan, but you can also focus on small actions.

COMMUNICATION

Just like with feedback and training, engaging staff is about communication. As a leader, you set the tone in your library, and what and how you share information with staff will set the stage for staff engagement.

Strong communication needs to flow in all directions to engage staff. Staff have to share with managers, managers with the director, the director with the board, and vice versa. Giving people access to information will help them stay engaged. Not every staff member will be interested in staying up to date on everything, but having as much transparency in the decision making and projects going on with all levels of the organization will help staff stay committed to the mission of the library.

When thinking about how to communicate, consider what works best for your library. Do you have regular staff meetings? Department meetings? Weekly staff emails? How do staff find out about what is going on throughout the library and within the community? Are they given the opportunity to stay up to date on what the board is working on by having easy access to board packets and the ability to attend or watch recordings of the board meetings?

When sharing information, be aware of who you are sharing information with. Make sure you have not cultivated favorite employees who you share more information with than others. Spread information evenly and without bias throughout the organization, and use the communication channels to reinforce the values of the library and share more about your own values.

WELCOMING AND INCLUSIVE

When considering how to engage staff, being welcoming and inclusive should be at the top of your list. There are some initial steps that you can take to make staff feel welcome:

- Acknowledge where you are at on your equity, diversity, and inclusion (EDI) journey as an organization and what your plans are for improving.
- Ask what barriers exist for staff in bringing their full self to work and what can the library do to help them feel welcomed, included, and valued.
- Develop strong policies and procedures on handling harassment, discrimination, and microaggressions in the workplace and then train staff on them.
- Hold patrons and other staff accountable when they are discriminating, bullying, or harassing other staff.
- Make staff workspaces ADA compliant.

- Offer pronoun pins/badges/lanyards to staff with their pronouns.
- Have non-gendered bathrooms.
- Create/designate a private area where nursing mothers can go.
- Offer an employee assistance program or other mental health assistance program to staff.
- Do regular trainings for staff on creating an inclusive environment where staff can bring their fully authentic selves.

Remember that people are all icebergs. You only see the top 10 percent of what they are about, and the remaining 90 percent hides under the surface. Don't assume that all of your staff think or identify the same way you do. Instead, assume you know nothing and start by listening to staff and learning what they would like to see in terms of creating an inclusive environment.

JUST FOR FUN

While learning is important, we also need to just have fun sometimes. Engaging staff and keeping morale high means letting staff blow off steam or do something silly.

- Have monthly or quarterly staff treats (be mindful of dietary restrictions).
- Have a staff party (usually these are done annually).
- Create spaces for staff to share stories, photos, and so forth.
- Offer book, movie, music discussions or water cooler chats for staff to connect on shared interests and hobbies
- Consider having part of your staff in-service day be something fun/silly/relaxing.

There are lots of fun things that you can do to boost morale, and staff usually have a multitude of ideas.

AWARDS AND RECOGNITION

Library staff do incredible work and should be recognized for it. Some libraries have annual awards given to staff, which can be great as long as it doesn't become a popularity contest. But there are regional, state, and national awards that you can nominate staff for to let them know you think they are doing a fabulous job. ALA has a list of professional recognition awards,[1] but there are also local awards from service organizations or local chambers of commerce. While not everyone wants to be recognized this way, some staff do. Even if the staff member doesn't get the award, consider letting them know you nominated them for it because you were impressed with their work.

Recognition can come from awards, but it can also come from within the library. While the employee's manager should be giving regular feedback to the employee and praising them when they have done a good job, there are other forms of recognition that you can put into place when someone does a good job. Setting up a system where employees can acknowledge the contribution or help of another employee that goes to the director, to their direct report, and in their personnel file is a cost-effective way to encourage staff to boost each other's morale and engagement. You can also set aside time in meetings (depending on how your staff likes to receive recognition) for people to do call-outs on departments that have helped them in the past month or quarter. At annual staff in-service days, think about honoring staff anniversaries and welcoming new staff who have started in the previous year.

There is no one way to engage staff and strengthen morale, but if you listen to staff, respect them as individuals, and look for ways to show you see them and care about them, you will be able to keep morale and engagement high and your patrons happy because your staff are happy.

APPLYING YOUR LEARNING: SEXUAL HARASSMENT CLAIM

Ross approached the library director to lodge a complaint against two staff who were harassing him. He shared that they had started making fun of him for mentioning he is gay. When the library director heard this, she knew it was a sexual harassment issue and had to be investigated thoroughly. The director took notes on what Ross said and informed him that she would be doing a thorough investigation into his allegations.

The library director called the attorney and asked for guidance. The attorney said to investigate quickly and thoroughly and change the shifts of the two staff so that Ross did not have to work with them during the investigation. The director checked in with Ross and asked him if there was anything else he needed to feel psychologically and emotionally safe. The library director interviewed the two employees who made the comments, in addition to staff in the department, updating Ross regularly on the investigation's progress. An employee from another department came forth, having witnessed the ongoing harassment of Ross. After a thorough investigation and discussion with the attorney, the library director suspended the two clerks without pay for a week and said that if the harassment happened again, they would be terminated. Moving forward, the two clerks were never scheduled at the same time as Ross. The director followed up with Ross to determine if there were any other actions the library could take to help him feel safe.

QUESTIONS

1. What is the primary issue in this scenario?
2. Who are the players involved?
3. What went well in how this was handled?
4. What should have been handled differently? Why?
5. What laws might come into play on this topic?
6. How would you have approached handling this scenario?

KEY TAKEAWAYS

Strengthening morale starts with understanding what your core values are as a leader and what your library's core values are.

Before you can strengthen morale or have employees feel more engaged, you need to assess the environment and hear what staff need to feel appreciated and acknowledged. While there are many different ways to engage staff and strengthen morale, start with making sure you have strong communication systems in place and have created a welcoming and inclusive environment. You can also consider nominating staff for awards and recognition and having activities that are just for fun.

Showing staff you are regularly checking in to see where staff are at in terms of morale and engagement will help you build a strong organization with dedicated staff.

REFLECTION QUESTIONS FOR CHAPTER 8

- What are my core values as a leader?
- How engaged are staff in my organization?
- Which staff are not engaged and why?
- What do we already have in place to engage staff and keep morale high?
- Are you listening to staff from marginalized populations about employee engagement and morale and acting on what you hear?
- What is one small thing I could start doing today to improve morale?

ADDITIONAL RESOURCES

Cloud, Dr. Henry. *Boundaries for Leaders: Results, Relationships, and Being Ridiculously in Charge*. New York: Harper Business, 2013.

Kaplowitz, Rachel and Johnson, Jasmine. "5 Best Practices for Equitable and Inclusive Data Collection." Charles and Lynn Schusterman Family Foundation. https://www.schusterman.org/blogs/jasmine-laroche/5-best-practices -for-equitable-and-inclusive-data-collection.

Lencioni, Patrick. *The Four Obsessions of an Extraordinary Executive*. San Francisco: Jossey-Bass, 2000.

North, Elaina. *The Six-Step Guide to Library Worker Engagement*. Chicago: ALA Editions, 2021.

Silverthorn, Michelle. *Authentic Diversity*. Oxfordshire: Routledge, 2020.

NOTE

1. American Library Association, "ALA Professional Recognition," www.ala .org/awardsgrants/awards/browse/prec?showfilter=no.

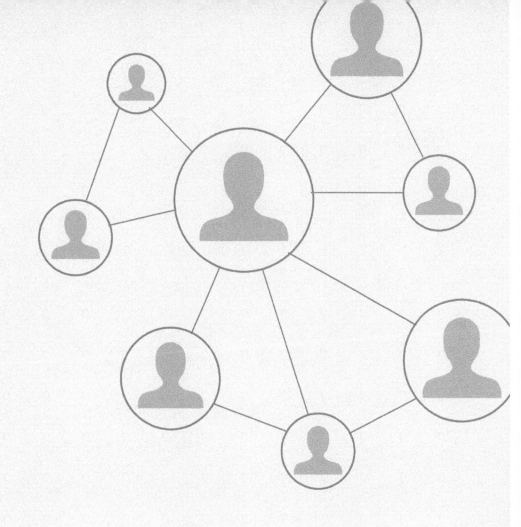

PART III
HR TOOLBOX
Depart and
Reassess

CHAPTER 9

Staffing Needs and Succession Planning

After reading this chapter you will know the following:
- + How to evaluate an individual workflow
- + How to determine staffing needs for your organization
- + How to create and implement a succession plan

||||||||||||||||||||||||||||||||||||||||||||||||||||||||||||||||||||||||||||||||||||||||||||||||||||||||||||||||||||||||||||||||||||||||||||||||||||||||||||

Personnel accounts for the largest portion of a library's operating budget, and having the appropriate amount of staff in the correct roles is critical to guaranteeing the library can carry out its mission. Budgets and needs change over the years, and libraries have to be flexible to meet the needs of the communities they serve while being conscientious with the funding entrusted to them. This is accomplished by evaluating the staffing models and workflows of employees and in creating succession plans for key people. This will help ensure that you are employing the people the library needs now, have a plan when employees leave the organization, and not lose critical institutional knowledge in the process.

STAFFING NEEDS

A library needs the right number of staff to carry out the goals and services of the organization based on the available funding. Sometimes, this means hiring additional staff for a newly created service. Other times, it could mean moving people to different roles within the organization based on changing needs. It may require eliminating staff because of a funding issue.

How do you know if you have too few, just enough, or too many staff? How do you determine how much work an employee or department can handle? The first step is to do a workflow evaluation and then a staffing analysis. When doing an evaluation or analysis of your staffing, bring the staff in as part of the process. They will have the best information on what they are doing and how they are spending their time. While people's perceptions might not be 100 percent accurate, getting staff involved in the process will ensure that staff not only understand what is being evaluated, but will also provide information to work with during the process.

WORKFLOW EVALUATION

Before determining whether your departments and library have sufficient staffing to carry out the mission and vision of the library, you need to first understand what work is being accomplished within your organization. This starts with strong job descriptions as discussed in chapter 1. Once your job descriptions are in order, having a master list of job duties like we talked about in chapter 4 (Onboarding) will allow you to determine the scope of the work being performed within the library.

Existing Positions

Once you have a strong job description and list of duties, you need to look at each position individually.

- Does this position have sufficient duties to fill the hours they are scheduled for?
- Does this position have too many duties for the hours they are assigned?
- Do all of the duties make sense for this position?
- Are there any duties that no longer need to be performed or can be assigned to someone else?
- Are there duties that should be handled by this position, but currently are not?

When investigating whether an existing position is right-sized, have the staff member fill out a log of where they are spending their time for a couple weeks. The goal of this is to determine where the majority of the time is being spent. This can give you a broad snapshot of where time is spent based on their various job responsibilities.

Then, looking at the duties list and job description, determine whether there needs to be an adjustment of duties, hours, or workload. Perhaps there are certain times of the year when this position needs more hours, or certain duties that only happen quarterly that require more focus and attention. Once you have a sense of where time is spent, you can better adjust for the position and overall needs of the department and library.

Vacant Positions

When a position becomes vacant, a good practice is to evaluate the relevance of the individual position. Some questions to ask are:

- Is this position still necessary?
- Are any of the duties redundant with other positions?
- Is this position for a service that may be sunset?
- Should the work be allocated to other positions?
- What will be the impact on the other members of the department if it were eliminated?
- Are there more duties than can reasonably be accomplished with the hours for the position?
- Are all of the duties and responsibilities still necessary to perform?
- Are there duties and responsibilities that are not being accomplished that could be added to a new position?

Have the outgoing employee go through their job description and estimate where they spend their time (e.g., 50 percent on desk, 25 percent on collection development, 10 percent on programming, etc.). This will give you a sense of what the person sees as priorities for the position.

STAFFING ANALYSIS

Once you have a good sense of individual workflows, zoom out to a department- or library-wide level to look at whether duties are fairly assigned. A staffing analysis can be done for several reasons, including:

- If a staff member feels overworked and you want to determine where they are spending their time
- If someone is leaving the department, opening up an opportunity to assess the department workflow and duties assignments
- If the work of the department has changed and duties need to be reassigned
- If a manager has requested additional staffing to meet demand for services in the department
- If the budget needs to be cut and you need to determine where to make those cuts

Before you can crunch the numbers, you have to determine where your library sits philosophically with the workload for staff. Some libraries strive to give staff time off the public service desk, while others do not give any or only give staff time off the public service desk to full-time staff. For some libraries, budgetary constraints play a large role in what they ask of staff, but no matter what your funding, every director should keep in mind staff morale and acceptable workloads when looking at staffing scenarios.

Determine what the main areas of responsibilities are for each department and what the targeted amount of time you want each position spending on different tasks. For a public service department, it might look like table 9.1.

TABLE 9.1 | **Staff workflow chart**

	FULL-TIME	PART-TIME	MANAGERS	NOTES
DESK	50%	75%	20%	assumes some off peak hours to allow other work to be accomplished while on desk
PROGRAMMING	20%	15%	10%	includes planning, performing, and wrap-up
COLLECTION DEVELOPMENT	20%	0%	10%	includes selecting, weeding, and merchandising
MEETINGS & PROFESSIONAL DEVELOPMENT	10%	10%	10%	includes internal and external meetings, internal and external committees, training, CE, and conferences
MANAGEMENT	0%	0%	50%	includes scheduling, training, hiring, disciplining, providing feedback, and evaluating staff

Once you know where you want people spending their time, you can compare it to where people actually are spending their time based on the individual workflow analysis done. You can also determine if this is where you want people to spend their time, and whether you have enough, too much, or not enough staff to fulfill the duties.

Once you have looked at the ideal versus the reality, you can determine whether you need to add more staff, reassign duties, cut back on services or programs based on staffing availability, or leave positions unfilled if someone leaves. A sample staffing analysis spreadsheet is available on our website.

FUTURE-PROOFING YOUR LIBRARY'S STAFFING

When forecasting the needs of staff for your organization, think about the current and future needs of your organization. Understanding shifting demographics and evolving trends will help you make more informed decisions.

How do you future-proof your staff? Think about how the library's staffing has changed in the past:

- Has our revenue been consistent in the past? Is there an expected increase or decrease in the future?
- What is the age breakdown of the staff? How many staff will be retiring in the next few years?
- Have you seen a decline in in-person attendance for programming?
- Are patrons using the online resources more than in-house resources?
- Are you doing any original cataloging, or is it all copy cataloging?
- What education level do you need? Do you need to hire staff with advanced degrees if the majority of reference questions you are getting are instructional or directional?
- Are there any services that you think need to be sunset?
- Do you have a new service you want to add? What are the long-term staffing needs to handle the demand?
- If unionized, does the contract allow for the flexibility of adding or eliminating positions?

Library trends change over the years. At the end of the twentieth century, computers became the norm in libraries, and we had to design our buildings and budgets around that need. The more in-depth reference work that libraries did in previous eras has changed considerably with the onset of the internet and widespread access to smartphones. Many libraries have removed the reference collection and added more specific spaces. In the last ten years, makerspaces became popular and are now common in many libraries. Ample study rooms have become necessary as people want to either work in a quiet, enclosed space or want to collaborate with others. All of these changes have changed staffing needs in the library. The future of library spaces and infrastructure of our facilities will continue to change based on those needs and trends.

INSTITUTIONAL KNOWLEDGE

Institutional knowledge is important in any organization. Just like with families, organizations have history. Future generations learn and grow from that knowledge and history. The curators of that knowledge are not just the directors, but managers and support staff who have been with the library. This knowledge isn't just the social history of the library, but the when and why things happened, if any issues arose, or the justification for why a decision was made. When these employees leave, how will you pass this institutional knowledge on to the next generation of library staff?

Libraries have official board minutes, and some of the decisions may be memorialized there if the decision were brought forth to the board. But what about the smaller, non-board decisions? Libraries need to find a way that will work best for them whether it is a spreadsheet with decisions or minutes from meetings. To move forward, honor the past while letting go of the emotion tied to previous decisions as you regularly evaluate services and processes to determine what still works and what doesn't.

Revenue, programs and services, facilities, and trends are all factors that will have an effect on future staffing needs. You may have to make difficult decisions and realize that you have more staff than you currently need, or that you need far more staff than you can afford. By always keeping the staff workflow, library, and community needs front of mind, you will make informed choices.

SUCCESSION PLANNING

A succession plan is a document that outlines the transition plan to replace key employees within an organization. A plan should have procedures in place for a short-term or long-term vacancy and include enough details for someone to be able to determine how to get someone transitioned into the new position. Use positions, not names of people in those positions, so that it is a timeless document and does not have to be updated every time someone leaves the organization. That does not mean it should not be reviewed on a regular basis for relevance and accuracy.

There should be a more specific document that accompanies the plan, which will detail all of the specifics of the position(s). For example, the detailed document for the library director would include:

- Where crucial documents are located in the building and online
- Banking/credit card information

- Board information
- Login/password information
- A list of key vendors: attorney, insurance agent, accountant/auditor
- A timeline of annual work that keeps the library running: budget, levy, legal filings, and so on

This document will have banking and other pertinent library identifiers and should be kept under lock and key and reviewed regularly for accuracy.

We will focus on the succession plan and transition of a library director. A plan should be made for any key position utilizing the same thought process. There is a sample succession plan for a library director and key information document on our website.

FROM THE DIRECTOR'S CORNER—KATHY'S STORY

Since serving as an interim director at many libraries, I have found that succession planning is not a priority. For the director's position, there is usually no clear-cut, easy-to-understand filing system, especially for electronic files. There is no easily accessible login/password information for accounts. One library had no paper or electronic files for the past three years. This makes it nearly impossible for the incoming director, or anyone else, to get started right away. The incoming person will spend unnecessary time trying to find information, which may or may not exist. It is necessary to have a plan for all key positions in how information will be transferred to new staff. Key staff should think and prepare for a time when they leave the library; they should be able to properly transfer the information they have to new people.

MORAL: Keep your files in order to help yourself now and your successor in the future.

To create a succession plan, determine the positions you need a plan for. The director, assistant director, HR manager, business manager, and other department managers usually need plans. Be sure to include special positions that require special skills that are not easily replaceable: graphics, maintenance, accounting, makerspace. Think about the things that are important for that position:

- Is this position still necessary?
- If so, who can best take over in the absence of someone in this position?

- If that person is unable to perform the duties, who should be the next in line?
- What do they need to be able to step in immediately and perform the work?
- Can they do both positions or will we need to hire someone on an interim basis to fill the vacancy until we can find a permanent replacement?
- What do they need from the administration to carry on with the work in this position?

Once you have determined who should step in for the short or long term, think about the work for that position. Is it necessary for someone to step in full-time, or can it be done part-time? If someone steps in full-time and is from within the library, who will do their work? In some instances, and for some positions, like the director, it may be best to bring in someone from outside. An external person can utilize the plan put in place as well as the staffing resources in-house to continue the work while a permanent replacement is found. Whoever is taking over, either in-house or externally, they should be compensated monetarily.

TRANSITIONING FROM OLD TO NEW

The goal of any succession plan is to keep the organization running smoothly and to navigate the successful transition from the departing employee to incoming employee. It is important to plan that transition period and be sure that the new person is getting all the information they need for them to get started on day one. The role of the outgoing director, or interim director, is key prior to the transition. They have to make sure that all the documents are available in physical format and digital, so the incoming director can access them immediately. Look in the Toolkit for a sample checklist.

When the new director starts, if possible, there should be a short (week or less) overlap of time with the outgoing director for training. This is beneficial so that the old director is available to help the new director navigate their new role and answer questions. The outgoing director should create a training schedule so as not to overwhelm the new director and allow enough time to get through all the data. Have written documentation so that the incoming director can have it to refer back to. Even with a slower-paced training, the new person will not remember everything, and having a document to refer to will be helpful. Find a sample training schedule in the Toolkit.

Evaluating your staffing needs and workflows, having a succession plan, and being able to transition from the old to the new is key to keeping your organization future-proofed. We have to evolve with the changes in our community. Assessing past trends, monitoring current trends, and watching for future trends will keep our organizations flexible.

APPLYING YOUR LEARNING: STAFFING NEEDS ASSESSMENT

A new director had just come on board at the Metropolis Public Library. Lois was charged with finding a way to be open more hours. For the first few months, Lois observed staff and their routines, learning how tasks were done. She made notes on what could be streamlined and talked to staff about what would make their jobs easier.

After six months, Lois had developed a plan. She knew what staff needed to do on a day-to-day basis and put together a list of all the required tasks and how long each took. She presented her plan to the board, showing how they could increase the library's hours. The board loved the plan and told her to implement it right away.

The next day, Lois shared the plan with staff, who were caught off guard and had lots of feelings about the plan, the chief complaint being that Lois was going to change the hours staff worked starting next week. Lois had been observing staff and had immediately noticed that most staff came in at least two hours before the library opened. Staff reported that they felt it was easier to accomplish things when patrons were not there. Lois knew that if staff were only in thirty minutes before the library opened, they could be open many more hours. This was the linchpin of her plan. By moving around the hours people worked, they could open the library an additional ten hours a week without having to hire any more staff.

Lois was confident that her plan was the right way to go. Her staff were not.

QUESTIONS

1. What is the primary issue in this scenario?
2. Who are the players involved?
3. What went well in how this was handled?
4. What should have been handled differently? Why?
5. What laws might come into play on this topic?
6. How would you have approached handling this scenario?

• • •

KEY TAKEAWAYS

Ensuring your library is not overstaffed or understaffed requires a workflow evaluation that lets you assess what people are responsible for and how much time it takes for various duties, and determines how many hours a position needs to complete their essential functions. Once you have assessed how much work needs to be done at the library, who is doing it, and how much time it takes, you can do a building-wide staffing analysis to determine if you have the right number of hours and skills in each department to carry out the work of the organization.

Future-proofing your library means paying attention to trends and local forecasts to make sure you are prepared for up and down swings. Part of future-proofing your library is creating a succession plan for key library positions that will help with transitioning for those positions in the event of an emergency or departure.

REFLECTION QUESTIONS FOR CHAPTER 9

- Does my library have a succession plan for the director and other key staff?
- Do I have easy-to-understand files and a place where important information is stored that is known to key people in the library?
- Do I need to do a staffing analysis because I am adding a new service or need to realign the budget?

ADDITIONAL RESOURCES

Society for Human Resources Management. "Engaging in Succession Planning." www.shrm.org.

Society for Human Resources Management. "Performing Job Analysis." SHRM Toolkits. www.shrm.org/resourcesandtools/tools-and-samples/toolkits/pages/performingjobanalysis.aspx.

Society for Human Resources Management. "Practicing the Discipline of Workforce Planning." SHRM Toolkits. www.shrm.org/resourcesandtools/tools-and-samples/toolkits/pages/practicingworkforceplanning.aspx.

CHAPTER 10

Legal Issues

After reading this chapter you will know the following:

+ What the key HR laws are
+ How to procure and when to use an attorney
+ What to do if sued
+ How to navigate other legal scenarios

⁣||||||||||||||||||||||||||||||||||||||||||||||||||||||||||||||||||||||||||||||||||||||||||||||||||||||||||||||||||||||||||||||

During the life cycle of an employee, library management works within the guidelines of local, state, and federal laws. Knowing and following employment laws are necessary to run a strong and welcoming library. Most library managers are not trained attorneys or HR professionals, while being entrusted with decisions that are legal in nature. By understanding these laws, you can create a safe and productive work environment for employees and prevent costly legal exposure to the library.

HR LAWS TO KNOW

There are myriad laws to be aware of in the course of working with employees. Be aware that from an equity, diversity, and inclusion perspective, many laws lag behind current practice. Best practice for organizations working to be inclusive is to consider where your organization values and the law are not in sync and then makes changes that will benefit staff based on your values. You can always be more generous than the law allows. Table 10.1 describes key laws managers should know.

TABLE 10.1 | **HR laws to know**

LAW OR ACT	DEFINITION	APPLYING THE LAW: QUESTIONS TO ASK
ACA www.healthcare.gov	The **Affordable Care Act** (Patient Protection and Affordable Care Act), aka Obamacare, states that large employers (fifty full-time or full-time equivalent employees or more) are required to offer affordable health insurance to their employees. Smaller employers may also choose to follow the act as an added benefit for their employees.	• Is my library required to comply with the ACA requirement? • If not, do we choose to offer the same benefits?
ADA www.ada.gov	The **Americans with Disabilities Act** of 1990 prohibits covered employers from discriminating against a person based on their disability.	• What steps have I taken to remove accessibility barriers for staff in my organization? • Have I treated all employees equally? • Have I assumed someone needed an accommodation who did not ask for one? • Have I engaged in an interactive process when asked for an accommodation?
ADEA www.eeoc.gov/adea-discrimination	The **Age Discrimination in Employment Act** of 1967 prohibits discrimination against people forty years of age or older.	• Do I treat employees of different ages equally?
COBRA www.dol.gov/general/topics/health-plans/cobra	The **Consolidated Omnibus Budget Reconciliation Act** of 1985 requires that employers allow eligible employees and their dependents the option of continuing their health insurance coverage in the event the employee loses their job or has a reduction of work hours.	• Have I provided terminated employees with the necessary information on continuing their health care coverage? • Have I given COBRA information to staff who are retiring? • Have I provided COBRA information to the spouse of a staff member who passed away while on COBRA or while working at the library?

LAW OR ACT	DEFINITION	APPLYING THE LAW: QUESTIONS TO ASK
EEOC www.eeoc.gov	The **Equal Employment Opportunity Commission** was established in 1964 as a separate federal agency that works to ensure employers comply with federal civil rights statutes. Any employee who feels that they have been discriminated against based on race, color, religion, sex (including pregnancy, gender identity, and sexual orientation), national origin, disability, age (age forty or older), or genetic information may contact the EEOC and file a complaint against their employer.	• What steps have I taken to ensure that I have treated all employees equally? • Am I aware of any unconscious biases that I may be displaying? • How is an EEOC complaint handled? • Are the library's workplace policies updated to reflect the changes in state or federal law regarding unlawful discrimination? • Are supervisors and managers trained to identify unlawful discrimination and harassment in the workplace? • Does my state have additional requirements or protections not provided by federal law?
EPA www.eeoc.gov/equal-paycompensation-discimrination	The **Equal Pay Act** of 1963 requires that men and women in the workplace be given equal pay for equal work based on the same or substantially equal job positions.	• Are all my employees being paid based on their education, qualifications, and experience? • Do I have internal pay equity among staff in similar positions with similar experience and education? • Have I done a pay audit to check for equity?

(cont'd)

TABLE 10.1 | **HR laws to know** (*cont'd*)

LAW OR ACT	DEFINITION	APPLYING THE LAW: QUESTIONS TO ASK
FLSA www.dol.gov/agencies/whd/flsa	The **Fair Labor Standards Act** of 1938 outlines the standards for minimum wages for work over forty hours a week (Sunday–Saturday) and creates parameters for youth employment. It also provides guidance on exempt and non-exempt and salaried status for employees. In addition, it includes nursing-mother and equal-pay provisions and the requirements for record-keeping involving employee payroll.	• How are our employees classified? • Have we done an FLSA self-audit to determine if our employees are all classified appropriately? • How many hours is our workweek? • Are we complying with overtime laws? • Does our state have different overtime laws? • Do we have a policy explaining how overtime works in your library? • Is our pay in line with minimum wage laws at the state and federal level?
FMLA www.dol.gov/agencies/whd/fmla	The **Family Medical Leave Act** of 1993 requires employers to provide qualified employees with protected, unpaid leave for medical reasons for themselves or a covered family member. FMLA protects an employee's job status with their employer including pay, benefits, and position.	• Do we comply with FMLA? • Do we have a plan in place for those who do not qualify for FMLA but need time off for themselves or family? • Do we have procedures for when a staff member requests an FMLA-eligible leave? • Am I properly displaying the required postings?
GINA www.eeoc.gov/genetic-information-discrimination	The **Genetic Information Nondiscrimination Act** of 2008 protects an employee from unlawful discrimination based on their family, medical, and genetic information.	• Are we protecting our employees' genetic information and maintaining their confidentiality if in possession of that information? • Are all my managers aware of GINA and have I provided training to ensure they know what to ask and not ask in order to not violate GINA?

LAW OR ACT	DEFINITION	APPLYING THE LAW: QUESTIONS TO ASK
HIPAA www.hhs.gov/hipaa ***be sure to check with your attorney to determine if your organization needs to be compliant with HIPAA as many libraries do not	The **Health Insurance Portability and Accountability Act** of 1996 ensures the privacy and non-disclosure of a patient's health status by "covered entities" (health care providers, health care plans, health care clearinghouses, and business entities). It also provides guidance to patients on understanding and controlling their health care information	• Are we required to comply with HIPAA? • As an employer, what are we doing to protect our employees' personal health information whether or not we are required to comply with HIPAA?
OSHA www.osha.gov	The **Occupational Safety and Health Administration** was created in 1970 to ensure that employees have safe and healthy working conditions. OSHA is both a law and an organization. The organization sets and enforces standards that employers must comply with in order to provide a safe and healthy work environment. Many states have passed their own versions of the act.	• Is my workplace a safe environment for employees? • Are employees receiving the information and training they need so the workplace remains safe and healthy? • Do I have all the required postings up and in a location, staff can easily access them? • Do I understand all the OSHA compliance requirements?
PDA www.eeoc.gov/ pregnancy-discrimination	The **Pregnancy Discrimination Act** of 1978 is enforced under the auspices of the EEOC. The act prohibits discrimination of an applicant or employee because of pregnancy, childbirth, or a medical condition related to pregnancy or childbirth.	• Have I ensured that all persons involved in the hiring process know not to ask about pregnancy or parenting plans?
Unemployment Insurance	A weekly benefit that employees receive when they involuntarily separate from their employer. Every employer pays into the unemployment pool for their state for each employee. The amount the employer pays will vary depending on state law.	• Do I know how my state handles unemployment? • Do I know how we are covered for unemployment and what I need to do when an employee leaves? • Does my state require certain notifications of unemployment insurance eligibility and is the library compliant?

(cont'd)

TABLE 10.1 | **HR laws to know** (*cont'd*)

LAW OR ACT	DEFINITION	APPLYING THE LAW: QUESTIONS TO ASK
National Labor Relations Act www.nlrb.gov	Section 7 of the **National Labor Relations Act** of 1935 protects the rights of employees to self-organize: form, join, or assist labor organizations, bargain collectively, and engage in other concerted activities for the purpose of collective bargaining or other mutual aid or protection. Section 8 (a) (1) prohibits an employer from interfering with, restraining, or coercing employees from exercising their section 7 rights. Libraries are not covered under the NLRA, but some states have statutes.	• Which employees in my organization are in a bargaining unit? • Have I read through the collective bargaining agreement? • Am I complying with all tenets of our bargaining agreement?
Workers' Compensation Insurance	When an employee becomes injured while performing a duty at work they receive workers' compensation. Every employer pays a workers' compensation premium with their insurance company for each employee. The employer will contact the insurance company to report a claim, and the employee will receive medical treatment and a percentage of their wage (different for each state) during the duration of the injury.	• Have I posted my employer's workers' compensation insurance policy information and claims number in a place that is easily accessible to staff? • If an employee suffers an injury at work, do I know the procedure for reporting a claim as the employer? • Have I spoken with my workers' compensation insurance carrier to learn what the typical process is?
Whistleblower Protection www.whistleblowers.gov	Under the auspices of OSHA, employees are protected against any retaliation by their employer by reporting possible violations of mandatory workplace safety rules and standards. Many states have additional protections for reporting various types of unlawful behavior in the workplace.	• Are my employees aware that they have protections in the event they report this organization for a (possible) violation? • What training have I done with managers to prevent any retaliation in the event of a whistleblower complaint?

THE NEED FOR ATTORNEYS

With so many laws to navigate, sometimes you will need to call upon a labor and employment attorney. Like most employers, complying with human resource norms and applicable labor and employment law is standard; we have new staff fill out new employee documents, get them enrolled in health insurance and pension/retirement plans, handle their time-off requests, file employee evaluations, and maintain recordkeeping as prescribed by law. There are times where HR sometimes requires the assistance of an attorney. Check out the Toolkit for help on when to call an attorney.

Your library may already have an attorney, but do they specialize in employment law? If not, it may be worth retaining one that specializes in handling labor and employment matters. You can have multiple attorneys from different firms, or one firm with various specializations. Libraries should consider hiring attorneys with local government experience because many local, state, and federal laws have special exceptions or exemptions for units of local government.

When choosing an attorney, be sure it is someone you are able to communicate effectively with. They should listen to your concerns and interpret the laws applicable to your situations. Do they ask thoughtful, thorough questions about the issue at hand? Do they explain the details of what they suggest and help you find a resolution? Have they clarified the issue, or left you confused about how to address the issue? These are all important considerations when hiring an attorney.

FROM THE DIRECTOR'S CORNER—KATHY'S STORY

As an interim director, I often have to work with a library attorney with whom I do not have a previous relationship and have not built a rapport with over the years. This has posed a challenge when filling in as there are usually a host of issues to be worked through. When navigating these situations, I try to be as open as possible so that the work of the library can be done as effectively and economically as possible. While I do miss the strong relationships I had built with my attorney when I was a library director, I am now learning to work with someone on a short-term basis, knowing that we both have the same goal: to help the library succeed.

MORAL: You may not have the opportunity to choose your library attorney, but it is in the library's best interest to work with them in every way possible.

You want to be able to explain the issue and your concerns. They should explain the legal ramifications of the issue and recommend next steps. They should draft any legal documents necessary and help you through steps in warnings and/or terminations. This should be done in a thorough and efficient manner because time literally is money when speaking with an attorney. Once your library has retained an attorney, you may want to ask them to review your organization's policies to ensure compliance with all local, state, and federal law. You will want them to provide periodic updates on any relevant state or federal legislation, including any relevant labor and employment law changes. You should contact your attorney for any HR-related matter that is out of the daily norm for your organization and immediately notify your attorney if the library has been served a lawsuit.

LAWSUITS

Like most entities, libraries can be a party to a lawsuit relating to a variety of labor and employment law issues. Although libraries cannot prevent all forms of legal liability, they can take proactive steps to avoid unnecessary risks by training employees, communicating with their attorney, and being cognizant of employee concerns. When the library finds itself in legal trouble, it should know about some of the common forms of legal action taken against many employers.

Filing a Charge of Discrimination: A current or former employee may file a charge with the EEOC or corresponding state administrative agency alleging discrimination in the form of harassment or an adverse employment action based on a protected characteristic, which can include discrimination based on the person's age, disability, gender, pregnancy, race, religion, sex, sexual orientation, or status as a parent. Charges with the EEOC and corresponding state agencies are only administrative in nature, meaning they have not risen to the level of a lawsuit. Typically, the agency investigates and determines whether allegations made by the employee have risen to the level of discrimination. If the agency finds discrimination, the agency will act in accordance with its rules. If the agency fails to find discrimination, they will usually grant the employee a right-to-sue letter allowing them to file a civil claim in state or federal court. Whether the employee continues the process is at their discretion. Keep in mind that there is often not a lot of concrete evidence in these scenarios, and the legal and emotional ramifications are not always aligned.

Workers' Compensation: A workers' compensation claim is a quasi-administrative action taken by an employee against their employer after the employee suffered an injury in the workplace. The employee must first sustain an injury related to their position and notify their employer of the injury. Upon notification, a claim form is usually completed and submitted to the employer's workers' compensation insurance carrier. If the insurance company approves the claim, the employee will be provided benefits in the form of compensation and medical benefits based on various factors. If the claim is disputed, the employee will have to file a claim with the state's workers' compensation commission to litigate the claim.

If you receive litigation documents, take a breath and read the documents thoroughly. Once you have read them through, alert your attorney. They will walk you through the next steps. Provide them with a copy so they can respond in the time frame allotted. Understand that most legal actions have statutory deadlines to respond to disputes, so it's imperative that you contact your attorney immediately. They will likely instruct you to not discuss it with anyone (except the board president) until the next board meeting, where you will inform the entire board, probably in executive session.

Your library should have liability insurance for this very occasion. Libraries are rarely sued, but in the event they are, you need an attorney and insurance. Be aware that if you are sued, your liability insurance company may take over the suit and impanel their own attorneys for the remainder of the lawsuit. Let the professionals work out the details—that is what they are being paid for.

TYPES OF LIABILITY INSURANCE CONCERNING EMPLOYEES

Several different types of liability insurance help with HR, dependent on your needs and what is required based on your location. The following are some basic coverages:

- **Directors and Officers**—D&O covers the library director and officer (board) in the event a wrongful act is committed during the course of performing their duties. It does not cover wrongful acts that were intentionally committed.
- **Government Crime**—This policy covers all employees including the director and board in the event a fiscal crime occurs.
- **Liability Umbrella Policy**—An umbrella policy provides extended coverage for your current policies.
- **Abuse and Molestation Liability**—This covers the library in the event of an allegation of abuse or molestation of a person in the library. Libraries have been purchasing this coverage since we do so much work with children.

> • **Cyber**—This protects the library in the event of a cyber-attack. It will cover the costs to recover data and the credit monitoring of all persons whose personal information may have been compromised.

Lawsuits take a long time. Sometimes several years. There are a lot of steps involved in the litigation process, from being served notice of the lawsuit producing documentation in discovery, attending depositions, and engaging in settlement discussion. Most of this work will be done by your attorney, who will provide you and the library board with periodic updates. Also know that lawsuits can be expensive, as attorneys are not cheap. They have an expertise that we do not possess, which is why libraries engage attorneys and have liability insurance.

COMMON LEGAL SCENARIOS

A number of other areas may come up during the life cycle of an employee that can be tricky to navigate. It is helpful to have a general knowledge of them and how to work through the process. Some may require the experience of an employment or labor attorney.

ADA ACCOMMODATIONS

As we've discussed in chapter 2 (Interview and Hiring Process) and earlier in this chapter, providing employees with reasonable accommodations under the ADA is a detailed process requiring care and mindfulness. Before you can even engage with employees when determining reasonable accommodations, make sure you follow these steps:

1. Make sure your library is covered under the ADA: The ADA applies to employers, including public employers like libraries, with fifteen or more employees.
2. Review your internal policies and job descriptions: Your library should have an accommodation policy. Check that all job descriptions include detailed lists of job duties and physical requirements to support an analysis of whether the employee can perform the job's essential functions with or without a reasonable accommodation.
3. Train your managers: Ensure that all of your managers understand the basic principles of the ADA, like identifying accommodation needs and questions to ask or not to ask employees.

4. Talk to staff: Implementing accommodations will often be visible to other staff in the organization. Talk with the staff about what an ADA accommodation is and what can and cannot be shared about the accommodation. The goal is to prevent a negative impact on the person with the accommodation.

Once these basic steps are established, your library should be equipped to address accommodation requests. If you learn that an employee requires a reasonable accommodation, you must determine whether the employee "qualifies" for an accommodation. To do this, you must determine (1) whether the employee holds the requisite skills, education, experience, and other requirements to perform the job, and (2) whether the employee can perform the essential functions of the position with or without a reasonable accommodation.

Once the employer determines the employee meets the essential requirements to perform the job but cannot do so without a reasonable accommodation, the employee and employer must engage in the "interactive process" to determine whether a reasonable accommodation is available. The interactive process consists of a "good faith effort" to engage in a free exchange of information and ideas by both parties to identify reasonable accommodations for the employee without causing an undue hardship for the employer. The Job Accommodation Network (JAN)[1] provides examples of reasonable accommodations for various disabilities. Information and ideas exchanged in the interactive process normally include the specific reason or reasons the employee needs the accommodation and medical information provided by the employee's health care provider to further clarify information provided by the employee.

Accommodation requests do not have to be in writing, but should be documented by the employer and kept in the employee's medical file. Some accommodations can be low-cost, like changing work schedules or allowing remote work options, rendering the accommodation reasonable in some cases. Other accommodations like purchasing specialized equipment or renovating existing infrastructure can be too costly, creating undue hardship for some employers. Common requests may include

- Ergonomic workstations
- Fragrance-free workspaces
- Different parking locations
- Scheduling changes
- Use of a service animal

Once the library renders its decision, HR should provide the employee with a documented notice of the accommodation. Finally, employers should be aware that situations change, and an accommodation may need to be altered based on the employee's disability or changes in the entity's daily operations.

When you provide an accommodation to staff, you are signaling to them that not only do you comply with federal law, but that you want them to be successful in their role and know that providing this will help.

EMPLOYEE UNIONS

Every state has its own rules regarding public sector union representation, but most mirror some or most aspects of the NLRA, which covers many private sector employers.

Fundamentally, a union serves the interest of union members in the workplace. Depending on your state's laws, employees generally have the right to engage in discussions regarding their wages, hours, and working conditions. Furthermore, employees have the right to work together for their mutual aid and protection.

To become unionized, a union must file a representation petition with your state's labor relations board. If enough employees demonstrate interest under your state's rules, the labor relations board will certify or acknowledge that union's right to represent employees by bargaining with the employer over a collective bargaining agreement, representing employees in grievance procedures, and facilitating claims of unfair labor practices.

Collective bargaining is how the employer and the union negotiate policies regarding member employees including discussions of wages and benefits; establishing hours of work; paid and unpaid leave policies; grievance procedures for employee discipline; and other working conditions.

By understanding the basics of labor representation, libraries can avoid unlawfully interfering with each employee's right to participate (or not participate) in union activities or lawfully interact with employees when discussing matters subject to the collective bargaining process.

WORKERS' COMPENSATION

As hard as employers work to protect their employees in the workplace, accidents happen. Workplace injuries are unfortunate but a foreseeable issue for virtually all employers. Many states have a statutory time frame for employees to report workplace injuries. Once an employee notifies the library of an injury, the employer will notify their workers' compensation insurance company. The insurer will then decide on whether the injury was work-related and how much in benefits should be paid to the employee based on the circumstances of the injury, the employee's wages, and other statutory requirements. If the insurer denies the claim, then the employee may file an administrative action with the state's workers' compensation agency to dispute the claim.

Employee injuries can range from a cart rolling over an employee's foot to an employee falling off a ladder or other injuries. Many claims result in a routine finding of a work-related injury, but in some cases, claims can be disputed because there's a question of whether the injury was related to the employee's work, the cost of addressing this employee's injury far outpaces similar injuries, or the injury exacerbated a pre-existing medical condition. You want to foster a culture and climate where staff feel they can come forward with these injuries early and have the situation handled appropriately.

UNEMPLOYMENT INSURANCE

Most employers are covered under their state's unemployment insurance laws. Employers contribute monthly payments to their state's unemployment insurance pool to be paid out to employees who are involuntarily separated from their current employer, including being laid off or experiencing a reduction in work hours. In addition, employees must meet specific requirements established by each state's unemployment insurance law and file a claim with the applicable state agency. In most cases, employees are ineligible for benefits if they voluntarily leave their job, are discharged for misconduct, or experience separation from their employer because of a labor dispute.

APPLYING YOUR LEARNING: A NEW DIRECTOR'S DILEMMA

Quinn was the new director of the Everytown Library after the director of thirty-five years retired. During her first month, she started meeting with staff, wanting to get to know what they liked or wanted to see change about the library and their jobs.

The first staff member talked about how they loved their job but had struggled for the past few years after a cart of books fell on them, causing them to fall and break their ankle. They still had occasional pain in the ankle and couldn't always work because of it.

Another staff member asked if they could talk about the ADA accommodation request they had submitted earlier in the year, which had never been addressed. They told Quinn that they had hired an attorney but wanted to see if Quinn would work with them on an accommodation.

A manager shared that one thing they wanted to see changed was scheduling as it was challenging for her since she had two staff members who could not work together. They refused to speak to each other after one accused the other of harassment. No investigation had ever been done and the former director had told the manager to not schedule them at the same time.

After these revelations, Quinn decided to switch to looking over files for a bit. The business manager had shared the pay data for the past five years. But when Quinn asked for a salary schedule, she was told there wasn't one. She asked for copies of the job descriptions, but they were all twenty-plus years old and no longer accurate. She started digging through the data they did have and realized that many staff regularly worked over forty hours but did not receive overtime. She also noticed that there were pay inequities among staff in similar positions. When she asked about how pay amounts were determined, the business manager was not able to tell her, but was able to explain that they had classified all of the employees as exempt so they wouldn't need to pay overtime.

Quinn made a list of all the issues and called the HR attorney and then the board president. Fixing these things would take a while and would have to be her top priority for the foreseeable future.

QUESTIONS

1. What is the primary issue in this scenario?
2. Who are the players involved?
3. What went well in how this was handled?
4. What should have been handled differently? Why?
5. What laws might come into play on this topic?
6. How would you have approached handling this scenario?

KEY TAKEAWAYS

There are key HR laws that everyone needs to be aware of including:

- ADA
- EEOC
- FICA
- FLSA
- FMLA
- OSHA

Every organization should ensure they have unemployment and workers' compensation insurance. Attorneys that specialize in HR are necessary to ensure you are complying with state and federal laws and help you navigate challenging situations.

You also need to know how to navigate typical HR legal issues including:

- ADA accommodations
- Collective bargaining with unions
- Workers' compensation
- Unemployment

REFLECTION QUESTIONS FOR CHAPTER 10

- What laws were you aware of and which laws do you need to do more research on?
- Have there been any employee lawsuits, workers' compensation cases, or unemployment claims at your library?
- How would you assess when to call the attorney when handling an HR issue?

ADDITIONAL RESOURCES

U.S. Department of Labor. "Workers' Compensation." www.dol.gov/general/topic/workcomp.

U.S. Equal Employment Opportunity Commission. "Employers." www.eeoc.gov/employers.

NOTE

1. JAN, https://askjan.org.

CHAPTER 11

Discipline and Termination

After reading this chapter you will know the following:

+ How to conduct a termination meeting
+ What steps to take when disciplining and terminating
+ What HR laws to be aware of during discipline and termination

||||||||||||||||||||||||||||||||||||||||||||||||||||||||||||||||||||||||||||||||||||||||||||||||||||||||||||||||||||||||||||||||||||||||||||

There are times when you may have to discipline an employee. They have gone through the onboarding process and have been given clear expectations of their role and responsibilities, yet the employee is not performing at the level that is required for the position; or they are violating library policy. There are times that discipline, and sometimes termination, are necessary.

DISCIPLINE

The administration should have a clear discipline philosophy for the library that delineates what issues or behavior constitutes a conversation, warning, performance plan, or termination. When creating your policies, you were mindful of being equitable and inclusive. The same thoughtfulness should be applied during disciplinary actions. Be wary of cultural norms that are centered in dress codes, hairstyles, or hygiene expectations and make sure staff are not disciplined for exhibiting their cultural norms.

Have members of the administration and managers discuss what types of reasons were disciplined in the past and what should be considered infractions in the future. Once the philosophy is determined, all discipline needs to be handled in a consistent manner across the library, ensuring that everyone is being held to the same standards and all applicable laws are being followed during the discipline process. Every person has the right to be employed equally and fairly by their employer and not to be treated differently if they happen to have a disability, be in a protected class, or have complained about a workplace violation. As discussed, there are federal laws in place to protect these rights that employers need to be aware of before they think about disciplining staff.

There are a variety of different issues that can predicate discipline. For some, being habitually tardy is a policy violation, while others are not as concerned with tardiness but are concerned with an employee who tends to ignore patrons and chat loudly with coworkers at the service desk. The key is to apply your discipline philosophy and ensure you are treating staff equitably when disciplining them.

Discipline should be done in a thoughtful manner. In the personnel policy there should be a disciplinary policy that outlines the steps of how discipline is meted out. Be sure to follow that policy as closely as possible. Generally, the discipline steps are:

1. Informal discussion regarding the issue
2. Progressive discipline model
   - verbal warning
   - written warning
   - second written warning/suspension/performance improvement plan (PIP)
   - termination

The entire process should not be longer than six months or so. That is enough time to work through the process and for the employee to show marked improvement or show that they are unable to make the necessary improvements. The longer the process takes, the more disruption to the organization.

When someone is violating a policy or performing below expectations, start by checking the library policies to determine where the employee is falling short. When they were onboarded, they received and read the policy handbook and signed off that they were expected to follow the library's policies.

For libraries that are unionized, discipline will likely be spelled out in the union contract. If the employee being disciplined is in a bargaining unit, be sure to review the contract and follow the process so as not to violate the contract terms.

It is important to catch and nip issues in the bud. Many people wait, or they never have the difficult conversations about unsatisfactory work or a policy violation. It is uncomfortable to discuss these issues with employees. Ignoring it won't make it disappear. The next thing you know it is a year into their employment, sometimes more, and the issue has never been addressed and is now impacting other employees or the entire library. How do you rectify a situation that has gone on for an extensive amount of time? No one wins in this instance; not the library and certainly not the employee. You owe it to them to address the issue immediately and to give them time to correct it.

On the first notice of an infraction, have a conversation with the employee about the issue. Explain how their policy violation or poor performance impacts the work of other staff and the library as a whole. Tell them how it needs to be rectified and what you expect from them going forward. Be sure to document the conversation to the employee so that they are clear about what was discussed and what is expected to change. Make a copy for their employee file, with the date and their response to your conversation, if any. Ideally this will be a one-off and the issue is resolved.

If the issue continues, a formal warning may be necessary, which is the beginning of the progressive discipline process. The library should have consistent standard warning forms to use. Find sample forms on our website.

PROGRESSIVE DISCIPLINE

When done well, the progressive discipline model will help the employee to improve and become a valued and productive employee. A key component of the model is to provide incremental feedback of the improvements you are seeing and areas where more improvement is needed to guide them toward success.

Verbal Warning

After giving an informal warning to an employee, it may become necessary to move to a verbal warning if the issue continues. Bring the employee to a location where other staff cannot interrupt or overhear you:

1. Discuss the issue, as you did in the informal discussion.
2. Ask them if they are getting everything they need from management in order for them to do their job effectively.
3. If the employee responds with something they need in order to improve, discuss how you can make that happen and what your expectations are going forward.
4. Be prepared to adjust your assessment or course of action if additional details or context emerges or if issues you were unaware of are brought to your attention.
5. Make notes and email the employee a summary of what was discussed.

6. Be sure to follow up with any needs that they have requested moving forward.
7. Check in with them in a week or so to see how it is going.

If this is the very first time that you have to discipline an employee and are unsure if the issue warrants discipline or how to go about it, contact your library attorney. After you explain what is going on, they will tell you if it rises to the level of discipline and will help you through that process. As always, the goal is to help the employee improve. In the event that the employee does not improve after an informal conversation and a verbal warning, a written warning may be necessary.

Written Warning

The written warning is a sign that the issue is not being remedied in a satisfactory manner and needs immediate attention. This is the point where you state that if significant and sustained change does not occur, additional disciplinary action up to and including termination will occur. There are times when an issue may be so egregious that it will warrant skipping the informal and verbal warning and going directly to a written warning. Your discipline policy should have a statement that indicates that while the library makes every attempt to follow the discipline policy, it may be necessary to skip steps.

The procedure for a written warning is similar to the verbal warning. This warning should be accompanied by the written warning form, stating the prior discussion and verbal warning. Once again, note that the issue needs to be remedied. Ask them if they understand what is needed and what, if anything, they need from you to help them accomplish the desired result. Be sure to note, verbally and on the warning form, what the next step is if no change happens. Depending on your policy, that next step may include a suspension, PIP, or termination.

Second Warning/Suspension/PIP

If the previous warnings have not worked with this employee, it is time to move to the next step. Depending on your policy, a second written warning may be the next step. This warning may be accompanied by a suspension with or without pay or will involve drafting a PIP. Some policies go from written warning to termination. Always do whatever you can to help the employee improve. The library should be invested in the ultimate success of the employee and take the necessary steps to ensure they have the tools and training to succeed. It will also be helpful in the event of a lawsuit.

If your policy states that a second warning is accompanied by a suspension, with or without pay, let the employee know that when they return, the issue is expected to be rectified, and, if it is not, termination is the next step.

PERFORMANCE IMPROVEMENT PLAN (PIP)

A PIP is a tool that can be used when it becomes necessary to have a more formal plan for improving an employee's performance. This plan is a document, similar to a contract, which is created between employer and employee outlining the work that needs to be completed within a specified time period by the employee in order to rectify the issue under discussion.

An improvement plan takes a lot of work on the manager or library director's part. They need to be actively engaged with, monitor, and check in regularly with the employee to support them during the process. This is important for a few reasons. One, it lets the employee know that they have support and the library wants them to improve. Second, it shows that the library is actively working with the employee to improve their performance and is invested in the improvement of the employee in the event of a termination and potential lawsuit. Be sure that the PIP does not have so much work in it that it will be unlikely for the employee to succeed in completing it. The needed improvement(s) should be in measurable increments so that they can be successful, not set the employee up for failure.

When executing a performance plan, there are several ways that this can be done. The manager or director can oversee the process themselves, engaging with the employee. This is the most common method, as the manager/director is familiar with the person and work in question, and can closely monitor the employee's progress. If the employee has had repeated warnings or is part of a protected class and you want to proceed with more deliberation, it may be best to bring in a third party to coach or mediate the situation. Of course, this can be an expensive venture and will be budget dependent.

Bringing in a third-party coach or mediator will allow any emotions or preconceived notions to be removed from the employer and employee's point of view. By disengaging from director oversight and managing the employee as they go through their PIP and having a paid professional take the helm indicates the seriousness of the employer to resolve the issue in a fair and equitable manner. A coach will work closely with the employer and employee, following the PIP and timeline to help achieve the desired improvements.

A mediator may be brought in when the employee is an employee who has had several disciplinary actions in the past, or they may be a long-term employee who is no longer performing at the level they had in the past. A mediator can set the tone, calmly go through the issue with all parties involved, and find ways for the parties to come to agreement regarding the work product or other conclusion.

A PIP should state the expectations for improvement. Also, a reasonable time frame for improvement should be included, and if the issue is not rectified by the specified date, it should state that the next step is termination. While this may appear harsh, you have intervened no less than twice, probably more, to work with the employee to perform at the level expected. Being very specific as to expectations for the position, time frame to rectify, and consequences if not rectified is necessary, not only for the employee to know that this is serious business, but also to ensure that the employee is not surprised in the event they are terminated. There is a sample PIP on our website.

It is important to note that you should take every opportunity to follow a progressive discipline model, but there are times when it is necessary to skip steps or even terminate someone immediately. As always, check with your attorney on these matters. The goal of a PIP, regardless of how it is managed, is for the employee's work product to improve so that they can continue on their employee journey.

DISCIPLINE IN EXTENUATING CIRCUMSTANCES

Employers should treat employees consistently and hold everyone account-able when applying policies and standards, taking into consideration any Americans with Disability Act accommodations that have been requested. If one employee is often tardy and they are not reprimanded, but another is reprimanded for the same behavior, that is not being consistent in applying policy. As with hiring, nothing should be involved in the decision to discipline an employee except their ability to perform their duties. While your discipline of an employee should be consistent and applied equally to every employee who merits it, you may have to handle the discipline differently if there are extenuating circumstances. As with any discipline, you still need to consider the impact of the employee's actions on their colleagues. This doesn't mean that an employee who may have extenuating circumstances cannot be disci-plined; it means that you may have to take extra care to make sure none of their rights are being violated and that they are being disciplined despite that circumstance.

Americans with Disabilities Act (ADA)

It may be necessary to discipline an employee who has a disability and has asked for an ADA accommodation, or if during the discipline process it is revealed that they need an accommodation. You cannot assume because an employee has a disability that they cannot perform their work in an effective manner—that is discrimination. If they are not performing at the level expected, proceed with the discipline process as you would any employee. In the event that an employee requests an ADA accommodation, you need to engage in an interactive process to ensure that you can accommodate any reasonable requests. This process will include, at a minimum, reviewing the job description and essential functions of the position, and may also include medical or other reliable documentation of hardship to perform some of the functions and discussion on how they can be accommodated without undue hardship on the organization.

Long-Tenure Employees

What if you have a long-term employee who is no longer performing well or is not learning new skills? Are they no longer pulling their weight because they are not physically or mentally able to perform their duties any longer? Are there possible underlying medical issues that are impeding their work product? If you have an employee who has worked at the library for some time and their performance is declining, you should discuss the needs for the position.

People do experience slumps or have issues going on beyond the workplace that can cause decline at work. As a caring, supportive employer who wants an engaged and happy staff, it behooves you to inquire if something is going on with them. Even if there is, you should be understanding but still proceed with the progressive discipline. Oftentimes, the employee is so wrapped up in their personal issue that they don't see that it is impacting their work product.

You may find that you have a long-term employee who has been labeled "difficult": they don't carry their weight, they have problems getting along with staff and patrons, and no one has been willing or able to discipline them for a variety of reasons. Instead of addressing any issues at the onset, the behavior has been allowed to continue, doing the employee, fellow staff, and library no favors. You cannot continue to perpetuate that any further and should begin the progressive discipline process.

Either of these issues can affect the workplace dynamic, morale, and work product of other staff members. Engaging in disciplinary measures when extenuating circumstances exist should be a well-thought-out and executed process. It is possible to discipline these employees, though it may be necessary to engage your library attorney on how best to move forward to ensure that you are not acting in a discriminatory manner or violating any laws. This will allow you to safely move through the disciplinary process smoothly.

TERMINATION

Termination can be voluntary or involuntary and refers to all persons leaving library employment for any reason, including resignations and retirements. Voluntary termination will be discussed in more detail in chapter 12 (Offboarding). For the purposes of this chapter, we will be discussing involuntary termination. After you have been through the many steps of your discipline process without sustained improvement, it is time to terminate the employee.

Terminating an employee is probably one of the most uncomfortable tasks a library director, manager, or HR professional has to do. A person is losing their livelihood, and it should not be taken lightly. Spending the time before and during the interview process to make sure that the library is hiring the best person for the position will reduce the chance of involuntary termination in the future.

Before terminating someone, the manager should ask themselves:

- How have I laid out my expectations for their role?
- How have I given the employee the training needed to perform their job successfully?
- How have I provided clear feedback on what they need to do to improve?
- How have I helped them in every way possible to ensure their success?
- For an employee in a bargaining unit, have I followed all the procedures in the union contract for discipline before getting to this point?

If the answer to these is yes, then they can move forward with the termination. If the answer to any of the questions is no, the manager needs to go back and ensure they have given the staff member the training, expectations, and feedback necessary for them to successfully perform their job.

Many people will hesitate on this final step, even if they have performed all the necessary steps to provide the employee with the tools to be successful in their role and told them what will happen if they do not perform at the needed level. The best thing for the employee and your organization is to address the issue in a timely manner and proceed with termination.

One of the most important aspects of a termination is to have proper and thorough documentation. During the disciplinary process you should have amassed documentation that will help support the termination. Write up one final document to add to that pile—the termination form. On that form, as with the prior warning forms, you should have documented the issue and need for remedy and noted any further discussions with the employee. The form states that the employee has not resolved the issue to the satisfaction of administration and that the final step is termination.

Your termination checklist, which we will discuss in chapter 12 (Offboarding), will guide you in the next steps of documentation and preparation for the actual termination. Of course, when you have to skip steps and find it necessary to terminate someone on the spot, much of this offboarding preparation may need to take a back seat to removing that former employee quickly and safely from the building.

Now that you have all the documentation ready, how do you actually terminate someone?

THE TERMINATION MEETING

Terminating is best done in a quick, precise manner. A termination meeting is not a time for conversation or discussion of the issue that got you all here. All of those discussions should have taken place during the discipline process. This meeting is about wrapping up that process.

Before bringing the employee in for the meeting, have their manager, HR, or another manager in the room as a witness to the event. Having someone in the room will also ensure safety in the event that the employee gets angry and potentially aggressive. Have two copies of all of your documentation on hand, one for the employee and one for their personnel file.

Write a script of what you are going to say and practice it. What you say, and how you say it, is important. You need to be concise and firm, but empathetic, in your delivery. While the employee has gone through the discipline process and knows that termination is the final step if they don't improve, most employees are usually surprised when they are actually terminated. When you are telling them that they are being let go, the employee will probably not hear everything you say once you tell them they are terminated. Or they will hear something completely different from what was actually said—one of the reasons to have another person in the room.

TERMINATION SCRIPT

You: Thanks for coming in. As you know, your work has not been satis-factory and I have been working with you to help you improve. I believe you're trying. But it's clear that you are not able to consistently perform your essential job duties. Therefore, we are ending your employment effective immediately.

We know this is difficult to hear and we don't want to make it any more difficult for you. Here is information on filing for unemployment and continuing your health insurance. Your last check will include XXX days of PTO and will be sent to you on DATE. Please sign this letter confirming that you received all this information. There is a copy there for you as well. We have a box that you can use to gather your things in your office now, and security will escort you to your workspace and then to your car. I need your keys and name tag. Thank you.

Depending on the situation, it may be a better option to offer the employee the chance to resign with a neutral letter of reference, instead of termination. If they are a long-standing employee, offering them an additional severance package, paying health insurance for a specified time, or granting them some other small financial benefit may help soften the blow. This will allow them to exit in a graceful manner, keep the employer in favorable light with current employees, and circumvent the library having to pay for unemployment for an extended period of time.

After you have delivered the news, go over the details of their final paycheck, unemployment, health insurance, pay, and so on. Have them sign both copies of the termination form and give them a copy with their documentation. Have the witness or security escort them to their desk to help them pack up their personal belongings and escort them out to their car. Have the person(s) in the room write a short report of what had transpired as a witness in the event of a lawsuit or if the state unemployment department asks for documentation of the termination.

FROM THE DIRECTOR'S CORNER—KATE'S STORY

No termination is ever the same, but some are harder than others. I have had two that were especially hard.

1. One staff member started having heart palpitations midway through the termination. We immediately called 911 and paused going over the termination paperwork. After the paramedics checked their vitals, they said it was not a heart attack, but that the staff member should not work for the remainder of the day. They told the paramedics they were being fired so that shouldn't be a problem. I had planned to stop the meeting and follow up with them later so they could go home. But after the paramedics left, they asked for the paperwork, signed the letter, cleared out their workspace, and left.

2. Another staff member had been on a performance improvement plan (PIP) that had been extended once already, but they had stopped making progress in achieving the goals. When meeting with them to terminate their employment, they started sobbing and asking why we hated them so much. They pointed at me and said I was the reason their children would starve. I had another meeting right after and canceled because I was so shaken.

Though I had done everything I could prior to the termination to help the employees be successful in their roles, these are still hard meetings to have. They will never go perfectly, but I was glad I had made a script and practiced beforehand so they didn't go worse than they did.

MORAL: You never know how people will react when being terminated so be mentally prepared for anything.

Depending on your library policy, you may allow or deny unemployment benefits, in the event the terminated employee files for unemployment. If a terminated employee files for unemployment, the library may be required to submit several documents regarding the termination to the state unemployment office. There may be a standard unemployment hearing if you fight unemployment benefits for that individual.

Don't hesitate to terminate for fear of paying unemployment or a lawsuit. It is better to let go of the person who is not performing than to invest the time and money to continue to train, reprimand, and train again in a never-ending cycle. Usually if someone does not improve after some intervention, it will likely never get better. It can be a drain on managers, and it impacts other staff.

People often ask when is the best time of the day or week to terminate someone. The best time to do it is once you have all your documentation in order. Consider the dignity of the departing employee and structure your plans accordingly.

What do you say to staff when you terminate someone? Inform them in whatever manner you normally communicate with staff, indicating that Jane Doe is no longer employed at the library, that it is an HR matter, and while they are always welcome to use the library, they are no longer allowed to have access to the staff areas of the building. If staff persist with questions or state that they were fired unfairly or without warning, you want to state that you do not discuss HR issues with other employees.

Disciplining and terminating an employee are never easy things to do. We expect staff to perform their duties as assigned, to the best of their abilities, but that does not always happen. When using the progressive discipline model, you are working with an employee, giving them every opportunity to improve. In the event that improvement is not achieved after the specified period, termination may be necessary. Knowing that you did everything in your power to work with that employee is vital.

HR LAW

There are many laws that can come into play when handling discipline or termination issues. Be sure to know what they are and check with your attorney if any of these are in play.

AMERICANS WITH DISABILITIES ACT

The ADA ensures protections for persons with "physical or mental impairment that substantially limits one or more major life activities, a person who has a history or record of such an impairment, or a person who is perceived by others as having such an impairment."[1] While there is no extensive list of what is considered a disability under the act, there is enough information in the act to make reasonable determinations. The act also requires employers to make a reasonable accommodation by going through an interactive process if an accommodation is requested.

PROTECTED CLASS

The Equal Employment Opportunity Commission (EEOC) protects applicants, employees, and former employees from employment discrimination based on protected classes. They are the organization that has the authority to assure compliance and investigate any charges made by prospective, current, and former employees, if a complaint of discrimination has been alleged.

RETALIATION/WHISTLEBLOWER PROTECTION

There are times when someone becomes aware of a discriminatory employment practice and alerts the authorities. The employer may decide to not hire/terminate or cause some other form of retaliation to the whistleblower for reporting the incident or practice. There are safeguards in place to ensure the protection of that person.

APPLYING YOUR LEARNING: EEOC COMPLAINT

It was discovered by library administration that Henry had been falsifying his work hours, getting paid for hours he did not work. This is considered theft of time. He was terminated immediately. A month later the library director received a lawsuit from the EEOC on Henry's behalf stating that he was terminated because he was a forty-three-year-old transgender man. The library director contacted the library attorney and sent them the complaint. The attorney asked for all termination documents and the backup timesheets that showed that Henry had falsified them. The library attorney submitted these documents as part of the library's response to the EEOC suit. The library also denied unemployment benefits based on the reasons for termination.

QUESTIONS

1. What is the primary issue in this scenario?
2. Who are the players involved?
3. What went well in how this was handled?
4. What should have been handled differently? Why?
5. What laws might come into play on this topic?
6. How would you have approached handling this scenario?

KEY TAKEAWAYS

When staff are not performing at the needed level, you as their manager are responsible for holding them responsible, provided you have given them clear expectations and the training needed to perform their job.

A disciplinary process usually follows these steps:

1. Informal discussion regarding the issue
2. Verbal warning
3. Written warning
4. Second written warning/suspension/PIP
5. Termination

Terminations, when necessary, are still hard. Keep them short and to the point and make sure you have all your documentation in order.

REFLECTION QUESTIONS FOR CHAPTER 11

- Have I done everything I could to work with the employee to help them improve?
- Have I laid out clear expectations on their job responsibilities?
- Did I allow adequate time between warnings for measured improvement?
- Have I treated this person as I would anyone else in this instance?

ADDITIONAL RESOURCES

Patterson, Kerry. *Crucial Conversations Tools for Talking When Stakes Are High*. New York: McGraw-Hill, 2000.

Society for Human Resources Management. "Checklist: ADA Reasonable Accommodation." www.shrm.org/resourcesandtools/tools-and-samples/hr-forms/pages/ada_accommodation_checklist.aspx.

Stone, Douglas. *Difficult Conversations: How to Discuss What Matters Most*. London: Penguin, 2010.

U.S. Department of Labor. "Termination." www.dol.gov/general/topic/termination.

U.S. Department of Labor. "The Whistleblower Protection Program." www.whistleblowers.gov/.

NOTE

1. U.S. Department of Justice Civil Rights Division, "Introduction to the ADA," https://ada.gov/ada_intro.htm.

CHAPTER 12

Offboarding

After reading this chapter you will know the following:

+ What tasks to complete as the employee leaves the library
+ How to ensure a smooth transition of the position
+ How to conduct an exit interview

||||||||||||||||||||||||||||||||||||||||||||||||||||||||||||||||||||||||||||||||||||||||||||||||||||||||||||||||||||||||||||||||||||||||||||||||||||||||||||

We are nearing the end of the employment journey. You have written a job ad and job description, interviewed candidates, and hired staff for open positions. Employees have been onboarded, trained, evaluated, and mentored. If necessary there have been some disciplinary matters that were attended to and now the employee is leaving the organization.

When an employee leaves an organization for any reason it is called a termination. People leave for a variety of reasons. Whatever the reason, when an employee leaves, a number of tasks need to be attended to.

THE END IS NEAR

Unlike an involuntary termination when the employee is not in control of their continued employment, an employee who voluntarily resigns will submit a resignation letter, stating that they are leaving with a final work date. The resignation letter should be accepted by the administration and filed in their personnel file.

PLANNING THE TRANSITION

There is usually a transitional period from the time the person gives notice to the time they leave—anywhere from a week to a month is the norm depending on the position.

This period of time allows for a smoother transition of the employee leaving. When someone is in the end stages of the disciplinary process and pending termination, there should be some thought about the transition in the event of final termination. There will be a period of time when someone will not be in that position performing the necessary duties and a transition plan will be needed. While you are working through that transitional phase, you also have to ensure that all the steps to offboard the departing employee are handled.

Having a termination checklist is a must. There is a sample in the Toolkit. This list will guide you through the process and ensure that nothing will be missed during the transition. Below are a few things to begin for the transition:

List of Duties: Once the employee has given notice, have them look at their job description and have them note what they spend most of their time doing, what they no longer do, and what they have added to their job description. Ideally you have current job descriptions.

Reassign Duties and Intermediate Training: Determine what work can be reassigned to other staff member(s) in the interim or what work could be paused until a new person is onboarded. If they perform a unique function, have them train another person on that work so the work can continue during the transition.

Pending Projects: Have them write a list of all current projects, work, and assignments that are in process or yet to be started and provide instructions to continue the work. Work with them to prioritize the projects.

Accounts and Passwords: Have them document any accounts and passwords in a secure location for any accounts that they are in charge of. Ideally these accounts and passwords should already be in the possession of IT and/or the administration in order to have control of all the library IT. Having a password management system for your library will help with this.

Financial Accounts: If they are in an administrative position and have access to library financial accounts or a credit card, have them removed from any accounts as an authorized user and get any credit cards from them.

Bargaining Unit Employee: For an employee in a bargaining unit, the union contract may stipulate how an open position in that unit should be filled and if the duties can be redistributed in the short term, while a new employee is being sought. Be sure to note the steps necessary and follow them precisely.

At some point before their last day, staff will need to be informed about the departure. Ask the employee if they would like a few days to alert specific staff before notifying the entire department or library.

TO PARTY OR NOT TO PARTY

When someone leaves who has been at the library for a while, staff may want to celebrate with them and wish them good luck in the future. This is especially true when someone retires. Ask the person who is leaving what would make them comfortable before any planning gets started. Some are fine with a party; some are not. If a party is approved, be conscientious of how it is paid for. If asking for donations, don't assume everyone can or is willing to pitch in. Some places have a social fund that staff donate to for these types of functions.

However, if the library plans to celebrate the departure of a long-term employee, make sure that the employee is getting the send-off they desire.

EXIT INTERVIEW

During the final week of remaining employment, meet with the departing employee for an exit interview after sending them an exit questionnaire. Doing an exit interview is an opportunity for you to ask them about their experience as an employee, what the library did well as an employer, and what the library could do better in the future. The interview is about fact-finding and learning how your organization is doing as an employer. Be open to any and all comments or suggestions and willing to make changes if the comments are warranted.

Some sample questions to ask are:

- How was your onboarding process when you started?
- Did you get all the training and education necessary for you to do your job and continue to grow in the position?
- What support did your manager provide to help you do the job to the best of your ability?
- Do you think the communication between admin and staff is working? Between departments? If not, how could it be improved?
- Do you see any overriding issues within the library that you think should be addressed?

- Do you have any additional comments or concerns that you want to share?

Take notes during the interview and have the employee review and confirm that they are accurate. File the interview notes in their personnel file, and be sure to note the relevant pieces of information that were shared. At a later date, review the information and determine if it is something the organization needs to act on. Keep an eye out for similar feedback as it may reveal a trend or something you need to address within the library.

TECHNOLOGY

At some point, the employee's access to the library email and intranet will need to cease. If the employee is terminated involuntarily, that access should be cut off immediately—before, during, or right after the actual act—so they cannot gain access to any files or documents and cause any harm. If they are leaving of their own volition, their access should cease immediately after their last hour. You will need to determine the best time and way to terminate access. As discussed in chapter 9 (Staffing Needs and Succession Planning), a succession plan should be in place for any department documents that are necessary for others to access after the employee is gone and for staff to access.

If the employee has any equipment—cell phone, laptop, tablet, hot spot, and so on—be sure they are returned by their final day. Depending on your state, you may (or may not) be able to withhold final pay from the employee for the cost of the unreturned equipment.

FROM THE DIRECTOR'S CORNER—KATE'S STORY

At one library director job, we were going to be expanding hours and opening up on Fridays and adding a couple hours on Saturday.

I gave staff a few months before this was going into effect so we could work out any issues that arose. One staff member informed me she was not going to work on Fridays. Thinking it might be due to existing commitments, I asked if she had a conflict. She just liked having three-day weekends. I told her that we were requiring all full-time staff to work on Fridays and that we would review the schedules in six months and see if any changes could be made. She said that was ludicrous and stormed out of my office and left the library. She sent in a resignation notice that night.

Unfortunately, she was the only person that had access to the library's blog, which we learned a few days later. We worked with IT to find a work-around, but it took significant time and energy.

MORAL: Make sure IT and administration have all the passwords to everything or, better yet, have a password management system to store all passwords and easily change them when someone departs.

DOCUMENT WRAP-UP

There are a lot of documents to complete when a person leaves the library, whether it's an involuntary or voluntary termination. Besides the federal and state requirements, you will also have some library documents or file updates to complete. You are required to provide the following documents and information to departing employees:

Flexible Spending Account/Health Savings Account

Employees are required to give the employee documentation if they have an FSA or an HSA. The employee may contribute to an FSA while employed, but when they leave if they do not use all the funds in the account they forfeit the remaining monies. An HSA is also a savings account that must be used only for medical expenses, but the account is portable and employees may continue contributions after they leave the organization.

Health Insurance

Through the Consolidated Omnibus Reconciliation Act (COBRA) employers are required to continue the employee's current health coverage, at the employee's expense, for a limited amount of time, if the employee so chooses.

Pension

If the employee is retiring and the library provides a pension, you must give them the information about collecting their pension. Usually an employee has planned their retirement date and will need to inform their pension administrator about their final date of work and pension payouts.

457b Retirement Plans

The employee may choose to cash out the plan or decide to leave the plan with the library and take it when they retire. They also have the option to roll into another retirement vehicle, which they can do immediately or at a later date. You need to give them the documentation about the plan that includes the contact for the plan administrator so they can decide how to proceed.

Unemployment Insurance

If an employee resigns, they are not eligible for unemployment. When an employee is involuntarily terminated you are required to give them information on how they can file for unemployment in the event they choose to do so.

THE LAST DAY

Here we are—the last day of the employee's time at the library. Double-check your checklist to make sure you have completed all the tasks. Have you:

- Had an exit interview with them?
- Redistributed their duties to other staff?
- Completed all the paperwork and given the employee all the necessary documents they need to leave?
- Talked to IT to make sure their access will be stopped at the planned time?
- Did they return all equipment issued to them?
- Did you get all account login and passwords from them?
- Did they give you all of the library credit cards in their name?
- Have they cleaned out their office/desk/locker?
- Has HR ceased direct deposits after the final check?
- Did they return the library keys, key fob, or access card?

Assuming you have completed most of the tasks, you have a few still to go. Meet with the employee one final time to wrap up the last few things:

> **Contact Information:** Confirm the employee's current or future address, telephone number, and email address so that their W-2 is sent to the correct address and in the event the library needs to contact them in the future.
>
> **Final Paycheck:** Depending on your state and how they are terminated (voluntary or involuntary) you need to provide information on their final payout. Some states require an immediate check if they are let

go. Some require payment within a certain time period after termination, but no later than the next payroll date. If the employee has resigned, there may be a little more time to issue a final paycheck, but no later than the next regular paycheck.

If there is unused PTO, that may be required to be included in the last payout. Again, this is dependent on what state you live in. Be sure to check your state's requirements on this.

AFTER DEPARTURE

After the employee leaves, make sure to remove the employee's name and terminate access from all locations:

- Staff directory
- Website
- Intranet
- Server access
- Phone extension lists
- Vendor accounts
- Payroll

As discussed in chapter 9 (Staffing Needs and Succession Planning), when an employee leaves the library it is a good time to evaluate the position and the current needs of the library before reporting the position.

Congratulations! You have successfully completed the life cycle of an employee.

HR LAW

This section provides an overview of key laws related to offboarding that employees need to know.

CONTINUATION OF HEALTH COVERAGE

COBRA was enacted in 1985 to provide for the temporary continuation of health coverage. Generally, COBRA applies to employers with twenty or more employees, but many employers comply if they have fewer employees. The former employee is usually required to pay 100 percent of the health insurance premium after termination.

UNEMPLOYMENT INSURANCE

A separated employee can file for unemployment if they lose their job through no fault of their own: involuntary termination, loss of hours or available work, and possibly furloughed. There is no set amount of time an employee needs to have worked for an employer to qualify for unemployment benefits. Each state has different qualifications and guidelines for those who can apply for unemployment benefits.

Be sure to check with your state to determine who is eligible.

APPLYING YOUR LEARNING: UNEMPLOYMENT AND ADA

For several years Jane's injury did not improve, and she continued to work with accommodations provided. She requested to work fewer hours over the period of time, taking her from full-time to seven hours a week. When Jane was at work, she worked according to her accommodations and did a great job. However, she often called off citing her injury as the reason. She worked one day a week and often called off on that day. Since returning to work, she was no longer on workers' compensation (WC) and used up all of her vacation and sick time. The library director did not know what to do. Technically Jane had a WC injury, but that claim was closed for the most part (the library still paid for all her medications); she was not coming to work more than she was, and the library could never count on her to show up on the one day a week she was supposed to work, causing coverage issues.

The library director called the library attorney, who asked the following questions: If Jane had not filed a WC claim, would she be able to constantly call off with no benefit time available, and not be terminated? Would any other employee be allowed to call off constantly with no benefit time available? The answer was no.

After the consultation, the library director terminated Jane's employment. Jane filed for unemployment because she was terminated for calling off, but said it was because of her WC injury. The judge found that she had not been terminated because of her WC claim, but still approved unemployment claims.

QUESTIONS

- What is the primary issue in this scenario?
- Who are the players involved?
- What went well in how this was handled?
- What should have been handled differently? Why?

- What laws might come into play on this topic?
- How would you have approached handling this scenario?

KEY TAKEAWAYS

In a planned employee departure, you can take steps to ensure a smooth transition. Having a termination checklist for when employees leave will ensure you don't forget anything. Perform an exit interview with the departing employee and make sure you have given them all required information on:

- FSA/HSA
- Health insurance/COBRA coverage
- Pension
- Retirement plans
- Unemployment insurance

Get ready to start the employee lifecycle again.

REFLECTION QUESTIONS FOR CHAPTER 12

- What processes or procedures do we have in place for departing employees? Do any need to be revised or revisited?
- Is my checklist thorough enough or do I need to add tasks?
- Have I asked the appropriate questions in the exit interview?
- What have I learned about our organization from the exit interview?

ADDITIONAL RESOURCES

Anderson, Brian. "Offboarding: What It Means and Why It Matters." Bamboohr, April 23, 2019. www.bamboohr.com/blog/offboarding-why-it-matters/.

Frase-Blunt, Martha. "Making Exit Interviews Work." *HR Magazine*, August 1, 2004. www.shrm.org/hr-today/news/hr-magazine/pages/0804agenda _empstaffing.aspx.

U.S. Department of Labor. "Continuation of Health Coverage (COBRA)." www.dol .gov/general/topic/health-plans/cobra.

U.S. Department of Labor. "How Do I File for Unemployment Insurance." https:// www.dol.gov/general/topic/unemployment-insurance.

Applying Your Learning Answers for Chapters 1-12

Read below to find out how we answered the questions at the end of each scenario.

‖‖

CHAPTER 1: Job Ads Misstep

1. **What is the primary issue in this scenario?**
   Ben does not appear to have the skills that are necessary to perform the basic functions of his job. Beth did not conduct thorough interviews for the position.

2. **Who are the players involved?**
   The players include Beth in HR, the new employee Ben, and the computer lab manager.

3. **What went well in how this was handled?**
   The manager came to Beth as soon as it was discovered that Ben had not demonstrated the skills necessary for the job.

4. **What should have been handled differently?**
   Beth should have included the job description in the job ad so that applicants knew what the minimum skills and job duties were. She should have talked to the manager about the skills needed for the position. When interviewing she should have inquired about each applicant's ability to perform each function. It may have been a good idea to have each applicant demonstrate their ability to use Excel or Word. Why? Had the interviews been more thorough and demonstrative, it would have been easier to weed out the applicants who were more highly skilled for the position.

5. **What laws might come into play on this topic?**
   No laws are at play, just best practices.

CHAPTER 2: Hiring for All Accommodations

1. **What is the primary issue in this scenario?**
   The lack of acceptance of people of different abilities is the primary issue.
2. **Who are the players involved?**
   The players include library director Lois, manager Perry, and Jimmy the applicant. Peripheral players include the department staff.
3. **What went well in how this was handled?**
   Lois wanted to attract diverse job candidates and started working with a company that helped place people with disabilities. She worked with Perry through his hesitation to successfully place a strong candidate. Perry did not do a typical interview, but instead provided an opportunity to show what the job tasks were and give Jimmy a chance to try them and see if he liked doing this type of work.
4. **What should have been handled differently?**
   There was no thought put into creating a welcoming environment for Jimmy or setting out expectations for staff on treating all coworkers with respect. Lois should have done some library-wide training on accessibility and working with neurodivergent individuals. Why? The employees exhibited their bias and did not treat Jimmy with respect, making him feel uncomfortable and ultimately leaving the job. Lois's good intentions ended up having a negative impact on Jimmy. Her intent of hiring a more diverse workforce ended with a negative impact on a new employee.
5. **What laws might come into play on this topic?**
   ADA and EEOC might come into play.

CHAPTER 3: Watch Out for Wage Compression

1. **What is the primary issue in this scenario?**
   The minimum wage mandate is causing an issue because the circ manager's staff will soon be making just under what they are making, even after many years of experience. The manager wants to make more money and be in line with other managers in the area.
2. **Who are the players involved?**
   The players include the circulation manager and director.
3. **What went well in how this was handled?**
   The manager did her homework by researching what other managers in the area are making, and had a number in mind when she approached the director for a wage increase. The director was open to the conversation

and explained why the increase could not be granted, and did try to find an alternative option that might be beneficial for both parties.

4. **What should have been handled differently?**
The library director should have found a way to make sure that the wage compression could be less than what it was and find a way to make the pay more equitable. It may not have been possible given the budget constraints. There may have been other areas of the budget, or over-staffing needs may have needed to be addressed. Why? By finding a way to make the wage compression less, staff would have been paid more equitably and perhaps the manager would not have found employment elsewhere.

5. **What laws might come into play on this topic?**
Minimum wage might come into play.

CHAPTER 4: Parent Leave Benefits and Nursing Mothers

1. **What is the primary issue in this scenario?**
Brianna resigns because she was not given an appropriate place to pump.

2. **Who are the players involved?**
The players include Brianna, her manager, and HR.

3. **What went well in how this was handled?**
They were initially very welcoming and engaged with Brianna, to the point of allowing her an unpaid leave of absence.

4. **What should have been handled differently?**
Prior to her return, they should have reached out to Brianna to see if she needed anything for her return to work. They could have then planned for an appropriate place for her to pump. Putting a sign on the restroom door telling people not to enter was not the best way to handle Brianna's request. Why? Brianna needed a private room, not a public restroom, in order to pump. HR should have researched and found a solution for her to pump in private.

5. **What laws might come into play on this topic?**
The Pregnancy Discrimination Act might come into play.

CHAPTER 5: Workers' Compensation Scenario

1. **What is the primary issue in this scenario?**
Jane fell while on library property and then needed an accommodation.

2. **Who are the players involved?**
The players include Jane and the library director.

3. **What went well in how this was handled?**
   The library director handled the possible injury quickly by inquiring of Jane what happened, and they immediately took pictures of the accident site and noted weather, knowing that it was a potential workers' compensation issue. The director was responsive to Jane's injury and care, and when the director realized that the injury might be permanent, she started the process to find accommodations.

4. **What should have been handled differently?**
   This was handled exactly as it should have been. Inquire of the injury, contact the insurance company, and work on accommodations. Why? Addressing the issues as they happen, and dealing with the issues, will ensure that employees are treated fairly and consistently.

5. **What laws might come into play on this topic?**
   ADA, EEOC, and workers' compensation might come into play.

CHAPTER 6: Pronoun Badge Failure

1. **What is the primary issue in this scenario?**
   A department manager required staff to add pronouns to their name tag, but offered no training or context, and then ignored staff making fun of the pronoun badges. This made a nonbinary staff member feel alienated and fearful of discrimination.

2. **Who are the players involved?**
   The players include Marty, the reference manager, and two coworkers.

3. **What went well in how this was handled?**
   Management listened to staff on what they wanted in the library and were open to creating a psychologically and emotionally safe environment.

4. **What should have been handled differently?**
   The manager did not put any thought into rolling out pronoun badges. They should have provided staff with training on gender identity and the use of pronoun badges, discussed with staff why they were implementing this, gone over talking points for how to respond when patrons asked questions, and made it optional. When they heard staff making derogatory comments they should have immediately addressed the issue and put a stop to that behavior. Why? The way they handled this situation was harmful. The manager was only trying to look inclusive without doing the actual work it took to be inclusive. They also, in their attempts to be more inclusive, managed to alienate and lose a nonbinary staff member.

5. **What laws might come into play on this topic?**
   EEOC might come into play.

CHAPTER 7: I Don't Need Anything Other Than My Degree

1. **What is the primary issue in this scenario?**
   Suzy felt she didn't need to keep learning and then wasn't aware of new laws.
2. **Who are the players involved?**
   Suzy is one of the players involved; peripheral players include fellow directors and the library board.
3. **What went well in how this was handled?**
   Suzy did not handle any of her work well—nothing was handled well in this scenario except for Suzy being terminated.
4. **What should have been handled differently?**
   Suzy should have realized that having a degree was not the end-all, be-all, and that continuing your education is necessary. Why? Laws, trends, and best practices change over the years, and it is necessary for any organization to keep abreast of those changes.
5. **What laws might come into play on this topic?**
   So many … Based on what laws were broken, the library could be liable for a number of different issues.

CHAPTER 8: Sexual Harassment Claim

1. **What is the primary issue in this scenario?**
   Ross was sexually harassed by coworkers.
2. **Who are the players involved?**
   The players include Ross, the library director, and two co-workers.
3. **What went well in how this was handled?**
   Ross felt comfortable going to the director with this issue. The director listened to Ross and realized immediately that this was sexual harassment and an investigation would need to be done immediately. An attorney was called for guidance and the coworkers' schedules were adjusted so Ross did not work with them. Once the investigation was complete and the findings evaluated, action was taken to discipline the offenders. The director followed up with Ross regularly, asking if there was anything that could be done to help him feel psychologically and emotionally safe.
4. **What should have been handled differently?**
   This was handled very well. The only suggestion we would have is for the director to lead by asking Ross if he was okay and if there was anything that could be done immediately to make him feel safe before calling the attorney. The director should also have recognized that it could have been a discrimination issue against an LGBTQ+ employee.

5. **What laws might come into play on this topic?**
   EEOC and Title VII of the Civil Rights Act might come into play. Some states have different LGBTQ+ employment protections that might come into play as this is also LGBTQ+ discrimination.

CHAPTER 9: Staffing Needs Assessment

1. **What is the primary issue in this scenario?**
   The library director found a way to open the library for more hours to the public, but neglected to bring the staff in on the decision-making process.
2. **Who are the players involved?**
   The players include Lois, the library director, and staff. Peripheral players included the library board.
3. **What went well in how this was handled?**
   Lois did not immediately make changes, but instead spent time observing staff and creating a well-thought-out plan.
4. **What should have been handled differently?**
   Lois should have brought the staff in on the discussion on ways to open more hours to the public. Lois also did not give staff any time to get on board with the decision, instead announcing the change was happening in a week. Why? The staff members are the ones who are working with the patrons on a daily basis and they need to be part of the process. If decisions are made unilaterally without input from the stakeholders or the people who are implementing the services, it can make for a very difficult work environment. Staff need time to adapt to new situations, and changing schedules can have a significant impact on a staff member.

CHAPTER 10: New Director's Dilemma

1. **What is the primary issue in this scenario?**
   New director Quinn discovered that the previous director did not address several serious employee issues.
2. **Who are the players involved?**
   The players include Quinn and several employees.
3. **What went well in how this was handled?**
   Quinn sat down with employees to discuss their job satisfaction and discovered several issues. By listening to each employee and preparing to take action, it showed that she cared and was interested in remedying the issues. She then called the library attorney for guidance on how to

handle the myriad of unaddressed issues. With so many systemic fail-ures, Quinn was also concerned about the diversity of staff and retention issues with staff members from marginalized groups. She knew that a lack of systems and structures often allows bias to flourish and wants to make sure she explores the impact of all of this on her staff.

4. **What should have been handled differently?**
Quinn did everything right. The previous director handled so many issues incorrectly.

5. **What laws might come into play on this topic?**
ADA, ADEA, EEOC, EPA, FLSA, and workers' compensation might come into play.

CHAPTER 11: EEOC Complaint

1. **What is the primary issue in this scenario?**
The primary issue is the theft of time by Henry.

2. **Who are the players involved?**
The players include Henry and the library director.

3. **What went well in how this was handled?**
The issue of falsifying timesheets was handled quickly upon learning of the violation. A notice of lawsuit was received. The director contacted the library attorney immediately and proceeded to supply the documen-tation that defended the position of the library.

4. **What should have been handled differently?**
It was handled exactly as it should have been handled.

5. **What laws might come into play on this topic?**
EEOC and timesheet fraud (FLSA) might come into play.

CHAPTER 12: Unemployment and ADA

1. **What is the primary issue in this scenario?**
Jane called off work on a regular basis, with no benefit time available, causing coverage issues for the library. Being that Jane had a prior work-ers' compensation claim with the library and had sought accommoda-tions, the library did not think they could hold her accountable.

2. **Who are the players involved?**
The players include Jane and the library director.

3. **What went well in how this was handled?**
The library director made every attempt to work with Jane by allowing her to decrease her hours and also allowed her to take unpaid time off when she had no paid benefit time available.

4. **What should have been handled differently?**

   The director should have been firmer on expectations of Jane and treated her in the same manner as other staff, holding her to the same standards the other staff were held to. Why? By giving Jane so much leeway, it likely was detrimental to the morale of the other staff. It was not fair to the other staff that Jane was allowed to call off regularly and they had to pick up the slack.

5. **What laws might come into play on this topic?**

   ADA and EEOC might come into play.

CONTENTS

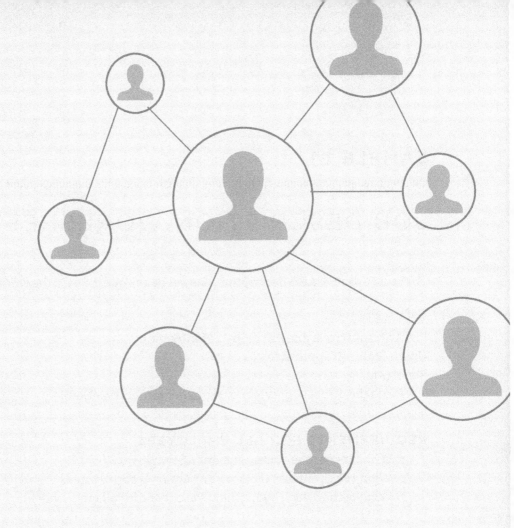

PART IV
Toolkit

SAMPLE 1.1

||||||||||||||||||||||||||||||||||||||||||||||||||||||||||||||||||||||||||||||||||||||||||||||||||||||||||||||||||||||||||||||||||

JOB DESCRIPTION WORKSHEET

To create a draft of a job description, answer all the questions in the worksheet.

Job Title
FLSA Status (circle one): Exempt   Non-exempt
Union Status (if applicable)
Reports to:
   Who is the direct supervisor or manager for this position?

REQUIREMENTS FOR ALL EMPLOYEES
- What are core requirements for all employees?
- What requirements tie into your library's core values?
- What technology requirements are there for all employees?

POSITION SUMMARY
What does this person do (1–2 sentence summary)?

REQUIREMENTS FOR THIS POSITION
What are the minimum knowledge, skills, and abilities people need to have to perform this job?

EDUCATION/EXPERIENCE
- What is the minimum level of education/experience needed for this job title?
- Is the relevant experience necessary or desired? (If only desired, leave off here and put in the job ad.)

ESSENTIAL FUNCTIONS OF THIS POSITION
- What are the main tasks or duties for this position?
- What amount of time (percent) is spent on each task?
- Order the tasks from greatest amount of time spent at the top to least amount of time at the bottom.
- Is this position similar to any other positions in the library, and do any of the tasks overlap with that position? Use the same wording for similar tasks.

PHYSICAL REQUIREMENTS
- What are the minimum physical requirements for this position?
- How can you reword the requirement to be more ADA-compliant? (For example, "Stand for four hours" could be "Stationary for four hours.")

SAMPLE 1.2

||||||||||||||||||||||||||||||||||||||||||||||||||||||||||||||||||||||||||||||||||||||||||||||||||||||||||

JOB AD WORKSHEET

This worksheet will take you through how to construct compelling job ads for your positions.

POSITION TITLE
List the position title.

POSITION HOOK
- What are the abilities and qualities that would make someone great in this position?
- What information can you share about the position that will draw the top candidates?

HOURS/FLSA/STATUS
- Do you need to list the hours per week or the weekly/monthly schedule?
- What hours will the person work?
- Are there requirements for working holidays, weekends, weeknights?
- What is their FLSA status? Exempt or non-exempt?
- What is their status? Full-time or part-time?

BASIC DESCRIPTION OF DUTIES
- What are the main duties of the position?
- What technical and soft skills are you looking for in this position?
- How can you convey what the job entails to attract people who really shine doing those tasks?
- Did you remember to link to the job description?

POSITION REQUIREMENTS
- Are you willing to accept candidates with diverse backgrounds who don't meet the formal education requirements?
- What are the minimum qualifications needed to perform this job?

LIBRARY INFORMATION
- What is your library's mission and vision?
- What makes your library unique?
- What are your library's core values?
- What is the community like?
- Link to your library's strategic plan.

COMPENSATION
- What is the minimum salary for the position?
- Will you list the pay as a set amount or a range?
- Will the pay be dependent on qualifications?
- What benefits does this position offer (vacation, sick, health insurance, etc.)?

UNION
- Is the library part of a union?
- Does this position fall in the bargaining unit for the union?

HOW TO APPLY
- What should be included when someone applies? Resume, application, cover letter, references?
- What is the deadline to apply?

SAMPLE 2.1

||||||||||||||||||||||||||||||||||||||||||||||||||||||||||||||||||||||||||||||||||||||||||||||||||||||||||||||||||||||||||||||||||||

HIRING PHILOSOPHY WORKSHEET

Before you begin hiring, your organization needs to know what your hiring philosophy is so you can hire people who encompass the values and goals of the organization.

Have every stakeholder who should weigh in (managers, board, administration) on the hiring philosophy fill out this worksheet and then use it to create a formal hiring philosophy that is in sync with administration, managers, and the board. This works in conjunction with the compensation philosophy.

PHILOSOPHICAL
- What is the library's mission?
- What is the library's vision?
- What are the library's values?
- How do we want staff to carry out the mission, vision, and values of the library?
- What knowledge, skills, abilities, and diverse backgrounds do we need to carry out the mission, vision, and values of the library?
- What is the role of our library in our community, state, country?
- How do we ensure we are removing bias from our hiring decisions?

PRACTICAL
- Do we prefer degreed professionals or do we prefer people who have years of library experience?
- Will we accept professional degrees from other industries (teachers, business management, etc.)?
- Do we want to cultivate a diverse workplace and how do we accomplish that?
- Do we prefer or require employees to be residents or live locally?
- How do we value work-life balance for our employees?

- Are we pro-employee in regards to salary and benefits?
- Do we value employee and departmental collaboration or independent work?
- How do we approach failure as an institution?
- How do we measure successes for our employees?
- How does the hiring philosophy pair with the compensation philosophy?

MY HIRING PHILOSOPHY
Based on the answers to the questions above, write 1–2 sentences on what you see as your library's hiring philosophy.

SAMPLE 2.2

||||||||||||||||||||||||||||||||||||||||||||||||||||||||||||||||||||||||||||||||||||||||||||||||||||||||||||||||

HIRING CHECKLIST

☐ Create a timeline for the hiring process.
☐ Review the job description.
☐ Determine key traits and skills needed for the position based on core competencies and the job description.
☐ Develop an interview plan based on position responsibilities and the hiring timeline.
    ☐ Create bias-free interview questions that align with the job description; equity, diversity, and inclusion; and any key traits or skills identified by management or staff in the hiring process.
    ☐ Create a scoring rubric to ensure standardized feedback.
    ☐ Scale the interview process and what you are asking of the candidate to the position.

☐ Create a job advertisement.
    ☐ Review the job ad and job description to remove any racial-, gender-, ability-, or age-biased language.
    ☐ Ensure that the job ad descriptions and requirements match the job description.

☐ Post job ads.
☐ When posting the job ad, use hyperlocal outlets (e.g., chamber of commerce, library system, etc.), national outlets, social media, ALA, and diverse divisions of ALA, such as APALA, REFORMA, ALA Black Caucus, and diverse job boards such as www.wehere.space.
☐ Review applications using the rubric you created and schedule interviews.
☐ Interview candidates with one other person using the rubric you created.
☐ Review feedback, notes, and information to determine who to offer the position to based on the skills and abilities.

☐ Perform reference checks on the potential successful candidate.
☐ Offer the candidate the position.
☐ Perform a background check/drug test, etc.
☐ Start preparing for onboarding as soon as possible.
☐ Select a buddy for the new employee from within the department who can be another resource for the new staff member.

SAMPLE 2.3

||||||||||||||||||||||||||||||||||||||||||||||||||||||||||||||||||||||||||||||||||||||||||||||||||||||||||||||||||

INTERVIEW QUESTION WORKSHEET

Sections A–E will take you through crafting strong interview questions. You can also use this worksheet to assist you in crafting the job ad. Use sections A, B, and C to ensure you have covered all the salient details in the job ad.

A. When determining what bias-free questions to ask in an interview, start by looking at the job description. Using one or two words, what are the main areas of work for this position (e.g., management, programming, collection development, etc.)?

1. _____

2. _____

3. _____

4. _____

5. _____

Based on the main areas of work, what specific skills do they need to have in each of the above areas?

1. _____

2. _____

3. _____

4. _____

5. _____

6. _____

7. _____

8. _____

9. _____

10. _____

B. What other knowledge, skills, abilities, and characteristics do you need someone in this position to have (strong project management, good customer service, data-driven decision making)?

1. _____

2. _____

3. _____

4. _____

5. _____

6. _____

7. _____

8. _____

9. _____

10. _____

C. What are key organizational values? (These are usually defined during the strategic planning process.)

1. _____

2. _____

3. _____

4. _____

5. _____

D. Create bias-free interview questions that align with the job description; equity, diversity, and inclusion; and any key traits or skills identified above. They can be grouped into three categories: skills assessment, behavior based, and values alignment. Depending on the position, you may have five to ten interview questions or upwards of twenty.

1. Skills

Skills-based interview questions are a way for an interviewer to determine if an applicant has the technical skills to perform the job. When creating skills-based questions determine the skills necessary for the position. Examples include organization, time management, scheduling, etc. When creating your questions determine what to ask that will showcase if they have those technical skills.

2. Behavior Based

Behavior-based interview questions are a way for the interviewer to get a glimpse into how a candidate thinks and behaves in a variety of scenarios.

As an example, one of the behavior skills you are seeking is someone who manages staff and wants to know how they handled having a difficult conversation with a staff member. Instead of asking "How would you handle an employee who was not performing?" ask "Tell me about a time when you had an underperforming employee and how you handled it."

3. Values Alignment

Values alignment questions are a way for the employer to determine if the candidate's values are in alignment with the organization's values.

Examples of values are:
- Integrity
- Collaboration
- Customer service
- Innovation
- Inclusion

E. Once you have crafted the interview questions, go back up to sections A, B, and C and make sure that you have a question that will allow you to assess whether they have the knowledge, skill, or ability listed. If you are missing one, go back to your questions and tweak until you are able to cover all the essentials of what you need to know.

SAMPLE 2.4

||||||||||||||||||||||||||||||||||||||||||||||||||||||||||||||||||||||||||||||||||||||||||||||||||||||||||

RUBRIC CREATION WORKSHEET

Rubrics can be used for determining who to interview and assessing candidates whom you interview. No rubric is perfect and so it is very important to take good notes during the interview process in order to go back and reflect on the candidate's skills and abilities.

WHO TO INTERVIEW RUBRIC
HOW TO SCORE
- **No Experience (1):** Did not indicate any experience/knowledge of key area.
- **Limited Experience (2):** Has some experience/shows familiarity with the key area.
- **Highly Experienced (3):** Has solid experience, mentions knowledge/skills/abilities that are at or above what is asked for in the job ad.

Reviewer Name	Candidate Name #1	Candidate Name #2	Candidate Name #3	Candidate Name #4
Do they meet the minimum qualifications? 1. 2. 3. (Yes/No/Maybe)				
Key Area #1				
Key Area #2				
Key Area #3				
Key Area #4				

Reviewer Name	Candidate Name #1	Candidate Name #2	Candidate Name #3	Candidate Name #4
Values Alignment 1. 2. 3.				
TOTAL				
Notes				
Bring them in for an interview? (Yes/No/Maybe)				

INTERVIEW RUBRIC

HOW TO SCORE

- **Weak (1):** Has little to no knowledge/understanding/experience of this area. Does not show necessary skills in the topic.
- **Strong (2):** Has a solid understanding and knowledge/experience in this area. Shows that they have navigated this topic in previous environments. Or shows a growing level of knowledge and understanding in this area. Shows they have interest in gaining more skills in this area.
- **Exceptional (3):** Excels in their knowledge/understanding/experience in this area. Shows that they have enhanced their understanding and knowledge of this area.

Reviewer Name:

Candidate Name:

Date:

Question #1	
Score	Notes:

(cont'd)

Question #2	
Score	Notes:

Question #3	
Score	Notes:

Question #4	
Score	Notes:

Question #5	
Score	Notes:

Candidate Question #1

Notes:

Candidate Question #2

Notes:

Candidate Question #3

Notes:

TOTAL SCORE:

Other comments on the candidate's ability to perform the job:

|||||||||||||||||||||||||||||||||||||||||||||||||||||||||||||||||||||||||||||||||||||||||||||||||||

COMPENSATION PHILOSOPHY WORKSHEET

Before you begin hiring, your organization needs to know what your compensation philosophy is so you are consistent in how you are marketing and paying for jobs. A compensation philosophy is a written philosophy that outlines how to treat employees regarding salaries and benefits and will help reinforce the library's values, ensuring the library is attracting, retaining, and motivating competent employees.

Have every stakeholder who should weigh in (managers, board, administration) on the compensation philosophy fill out this worksheet and then use it to create a formal compensation philosophy that is in sync with administration, managers, and the board. This works in conjunction with the hiring philosophy.

PHILOSOPHICAL
- What is the library's mission?
- What is the library's vision?
- What are the library's values?
- How do we apply the mission, vision, and values to compensation?
- How do the compensation and benefits we offer reflect our values as an organization?
- How do we ensure the compensation of the library is being equitably applied to all employees?
- How do we ensure we are removing bias from our compensation decisions?

PRACTICAL
- Regarding salaries, does the library want to be ahead of the market? Lagging? On target?
- What benefits can we offer employees to help with retention?

- Do we want to focus on a robust benefits package or higher salaries if we can't do both?
- What is the library able to afford in terms of salaries?
- What are similar positions in our community paying?
- How are we reflecting the library's values in the compensation package?
- Is the compensation package equitable for all employees?
- Does the compensation philosophy comply with all legal requirements?
- How do we address increases and years of service?

MY COMPENSATION PHILOSOPHY

Based on the answers to the questions above, write 1–2 sentences on what you see as your library's compensation philosophy.

SAMPLE 5.1

||||||||||||||||||||||||||||||||||||||||||||||||||||||||||||||||||||||||||||||||||||||||||||||||||||||||||||||

MANAGER ONBOARDING CHECKLIST

Employee Name: _____   Department: _____

Position: _____   Date of Hire: _____

BEFORE

- ☐ Perform background check.
- ☐ Send offer letter.
- ☐ Take down job posting.
- ☐ Create personnel file, evaluation file, and medical file.
- ☐ Update organizational chart.
- ☐ Prepare new hire packet.
    - ☐ Parking instructions
    - ☐ Telephone setup instructions
    - ☐ Timesheets/clocking in and out instructions
    - ☐ Computer login and email setup instructions
    - ☐ Organizational chart
    - ☐ Break and meal guidelines
    - ☐ Forms
    - ☐ Employee handbook

- ☐ Create email and computer accounts, add to email lists.
- ☐ Create welcome sign for work area.
- ☐ Assign a buddy.
- ☐ Create label for mailbox.
- ☐ Enter into time clock, create timesheets.
- ☐ Email employee with first-day information.
- ☐ Add to regional library system database.

FIRST DAY

- ☐ Go through new hire paperwork with employee (check off when forms are completed and returned):
    - ☐ W-4 and state tax forms (before first paycheck)
    - ☐ I-9 form (within three days of hire)
    - ☐ Emergency contact form (first day)
    - ☐ Direct deposit form (before first paycheck if desired)
    - ☐ Employee handbook
    - ☐ Name tag/business card form
    - ☐ Benefit (medical, dental, vision, etc.) forms
    - ☐ Take picture of new employee for employee photo directory
    - ☐ 457b account
    - ☐ Pension

- ☐ Issue keys/alarm code/key fob/etc.
- ☐ Issue library card or change library card status to employee if current patron.
- ☐ Take new employee on tour.
- ☐ Email employee location of staff photo directory, form finder, and online paycheck stubs.
- ☐ Call IT to help employee set up computer, phone, email.

FIRST WEEK

- ☐ Process all new hire paperwork.
- ☐ Add to medical insurance.
- ☐ Add to life insurance.
- ☐ Add to flex spending/HSA/HRA.
- ☐ Enter medical/dental/life coverage (or waive coverage).
- ☐ Upload picture into staff photo directory.
- ☐ Print picture and hang in staff lounge.
- ☐ Add to payroll system.
- ☐ Order name tag.
- ☐ Enter into new hire report.

SAMPLE 5.2

|||||||||||||||||||||||||||||||||||||||||||||||||||||||||||||||||||||||||||||||||||||||||||||||||||||||||||||||||||||||||||||||||||||||||||

MANAGER TRAINING CHECKLIST

OVERVIEW
- ☐ Your first year (focusing on learning)
- ☐ Review manager job description
- ☐ Communication styles
- ☐ Job expectations
- ☐ Strategic plan
- ☐ Facility plan
- ☐ Budget review
- ☐ Review annual timeline of events and deadlines

PERSONNEL
- ☐ New manager training on HR laws and best practice
- ☐ Review employee handbook and go over key policies
- ☐ Explain FLSA, FMLA, ADA processes
- ☐ Approve timesheets
- ☐ Employee evaluations
- ☐ Provide feedback
- ☐ Discuss handling discipline issues

POLICIES AND PROCEDURES
- ☐ General policy review
- ☐ Collection development policy review
- ☐ Department procedures review
- ☐ Library-wide procedures review
- ☐ Emergency procedures review
- ☐ Records retention procedures

GETTING TO KNOW US—TOUR OF THE DEPARTMENT AND OVERVIEW OF WHAT EACH DEPARTMENT DOES

- ☐ Administration tour
- ☐ Adult services tour
- ☐ Circulation tour
- ☐ IT tour
- ☐ Maintenance tour (security/building)
- ☐ Technical services tour
- ☐ Youth services tour

PROFESSIONAL DEVELOPMENT

- ☐ Attending CE for yourself
- ☐ Sending staff to conferences/workshops/etc.
- ☐ Reimbursing costs
- ☐ Joining professional organizations

TECHNOLOGY

- ☐ ILS logins and permissions
- ☐ Email setup
- ☐ Digital file storage
- ☐ Password management system
- ☐ Online resources and software for staff (event booking, room management, technology request)
- ☐ Online resources for patrons (event management, study room booking, etc.)

SAMPLE 6.1

||||||||||||||||||||||||||||||||||||||||||||||||||||||||||||||||||||||||||||||||||||||||||||||||||||||||||||||||||

COMMUNICATION STYLES WORKSHEET

When a new manager or a new employee is hired, use this worksheet to discuss communication styles and how each person likes to receive information.

	You	Your Employee
How do you like to get information?	Email Text/chat In person	Email Text/chat In person
• In general		
• Project updates		
• Feedback		
• Questions		
• Actions needed		
How do you process information?	Internally Externally Combo	Internally Externally Combo
How long do you need to process information?		
How much information do you expect from staff?		
• In general		
• Project updates		
• Feedback		
• Actions needed		
• Other		
What level of communication does your employee expect from you as a manager?		

REFLECTION QUESTIONS
- What do you need to focus on to ensure good communication between manager and employee based on the answers above?
- How will you identify when communication barriers/issues arise between you and your employee?

SAMPLE 6.2

||||||||||||||||||||||||||||||||||||||||||||||||||||||||||||||||||||||||||||||||||||||||||||||||||||||||||||||||||||||

SMART GOALS WORKSHEET

Write down your initial goal and define how it can be SMART. Once you have completed this, combine all the parts together to make your SMART goal.

EXISTING GOAL:

Specific	Who? What? When? Where? Why?
Measurable	How will I know when the goal has been completed/accomplished?
Achievable	Is this goal reasonable? Can it be carried out? How?
Relevant	How does this tie into your job? How does it tie into the overarching goals of the library (i.e., strategic plan, mission, vision, etc.)?
Time-bound	What is the time frame for completing this goal? What, if any, are the major project milestones?

SMART GOAL:

SAMPLE 7.1

|||||||||||||||||||||||||||||||||||||||||||||||||||||||||||||||||||||||||||||||||||||||||||||||||||||||||||||||||||||

TRAINING FRAMEWORK REFLECTION SHEET

Fill out this worksheet for any training sessions you or an employee are going to attend to help better process what is learned in the training and how it can be applied to the job.

Employee Name:

Date:

Training Title:

PRE-TRAINING
- Why are you interested in attending?
- What do you hope to learn?

DURING TRAINING
- What are the key takeaways from the training?

POST-TRAINING
- Did the training cover what you hoped it would?
- How will you apply (if applicable) what you learned to your work?
- What can/should be shared with other staff/departments/library?

FURTHER REFLECTION
- (3–6 months out) Have you applied what you learned in training?
- What other training would help expand on what you learned?

||||||||||||||||||||||||||||||||||||||||||||||||||||||||||||||||||||||||||||||||||||||||||||||||||||||||||

CORE VALUES WORKSHEET

In order to lead effectively, you need to know what your core values are. This worksheet will help you define what your individual core values are and how they align with your organization's values.

ANSWER

- Think about the moments you are most proud of. What made you proud and what values were at play?
- Conversely, think about the moments that bothered you. Why did you feel that way? What values were at play?
- Who is important in your life? Why? How would you define their core values?
- What is your definition of success?
- What are the issues/topics/items that you will not budge on?
- When do you feel really "on" and when do you feel "off"? What separates the two?

REFLECT

- What themes are represented in the answers from above?
- What do your answers show about what is important to you?

DEFINE: YOUR CORE VALUES

- List 3–5 words that reflect the themes highlighted in your answers above. These are your core values.

ALIGN

How do your core values align with your library's mission, vision, and core values?

SAMPLE 9.1

||||||||||||||||||||||||||||||||||||||||||||||||||||||||||||||||||||||||||||||||||||||||||||||||||||||||||||||||||||||

DIRECTOR SUCCESSION PLANNING CHECKLIST

DOCUMENTS TO GATHER PRIOR TO THE DEPARTURE OF THE OUTGOING DIRECTOR
PERSONNEL
- ☐ Succession plan
- ☐ Organization chart
- ☐ Personnel policies
- ☐ Procedure manuals
- ☐ Staff list (department, contacts, positions, status, salary)
- ☐ Salary schedule
- ☐ Job descriptions
- ☐ Job duties
- ☐ I-9 files
- ☐ Medical files
- ☐ Personnel files (including previous evaluations)
- ☐ Health insurance
- ☐ Pension information
- ☐ Union contract

BOARD
- ☐ Contact information (name, term of office, committee assignments)
- ☐ Board bylaws and library policies
- ☐ Board minutes
- ☐ Records retention documents
- ☐ Annual timeline of tasks/events/deadlines
- ☐ Strategic plan
- ☐ Current projects list

- ☐ Policies (board bylaws, general library, personnel, collection development)
- ☐ Attorney info (when to use them, current/pending/past lawsuits)

FINANCES

- ☐ Budgets (current, past, and supporting documentation on how data is gathered)
- ☐ Monthly financials
- ☐ Audits
- ☐ Bond information and bond disclosure documents
- ☐ Account login info for electronic access (include security question answers)
- ☐ Banking/credit card information (include documentation to change signatories)
- ☐ Internal controls procedures
- ☐ Outside account contact information and procedures (if applicable)

BUILDING

- ☐ Capital improvement plan
- ☐ Master building plan
- ☐ Emergency plan
- ☐ Blueprints (original, as-builts, renovations, print and digital copies)
- ☐ Vendor contacts
- ☐ Contracts database
- ☐ Liability insurance policy and contact/claims information
- ☐ FFE documents and depreciation schedules

TECHNOLOGY

- ☐ Technology replacement plan
- ☐ Inventory list
- ☐ Login/passwords list
- ☐ Website/social media login/passwords and procedures information

COMMUNITY

- ☐ Community leaders (include contact information for key administrators, legislators, and other community dignitaries)
- ☐ Local community group contact information (service clubs, chamber of commerce, places of worship, other organizations)
- ☐ List of annual community events
- ☐ Library networking information and any director meetups

TRAINING CHECKLIST AND TOPICS TO DISCUSS/REVIEW WITH THE INCOMING DIRECTOR

GENERAL

- ☐ Training schedule
- ☐ New director overview letter—explain where to access key info

MEETINGS

- ☐ Meet with each staff member (and union stewards if applicable)
- ☐ Meet with HR (if applicable) to review duties and key responsibilities of director vs. HR
- ☐ Meet with each board member individually and then as a group
- ☐ Meet with key community people (school superintendents, police, fire, mayor/local officials)
- ☐ Meet with library attorney (review any current/pending/past lawsuits)
- ☐ Meet with major building vendors (mechanical, plumbing, fire protection, HVAC)
- ☐ Meet with other vendors (insurance, collections, IT, attorney, accountant/auditor)
- ☐ Meet with other local directors
- ☐ Meet with local, state, and federal legislators

PERSONNEL

- ☐ Where are evaluations/disciplinary/"atta-boy" documents
- ☐ Review current staff issues including PIPs
- ☐ Location of electronic staff files
- ☐ Current staff projects
- ☐ Union contract

FINANCIALS

- ☐ Review all bank account/credit cards and set up transition of signatories
- ☐ Review invoice payment process from receipt to board approval to mailing payment
- ☐ Go over any grants that have been applied for/been received/ recently closed
- ☐ Discuss the budget and tax levy process and timeline
- ☐ Go over the monthly financials
- ☐ Review the annual audit and introduce new director to auditor
- ☐ Provide bond information and bond disclosure documents

BOARD/LEGAL

- ☐ Overview of board members
- ☐ Board packet timeline and preparation
- ☐ Current projects and pending projects
- ☐ Strategic plan review
- ☐ Past, pending, current lawsuits
- ☐ Review major board decisions
- ☐ Review how minutes are taken and where all legal documents are kept

BUILDING

- ☐ Walk-through of building and grounds (review where all key shutoffs are and how services come into the building)
- ☐ Blueprints/as-builts
- ☐ Capital improvement and master plan review
- ☐ Emergency plan review
- ☐ Emergency procedures walk-through
- ☐ Furniture, fixtures, and equipment (FFE) and depreciation schedule

TECHNOLOGY

- ☐ Walk-through of server room
- ☐ Equipment inventory list
- ☐ Login/passwords
- ☐ Website/social media login information
- ☐ Technology plan review

COMMUNITY

- ☐ Local contact information
- ☐ Annual events and library participation
- ☐ Library networking groups

WHEN TO CALL AN ATTORNEY

Not sure when to call an attorney? Answer these questions to learn when to call an attorney.

Have you encountered this situation previously?	Yes (1)	Maybe (2)	No (3)
Is there a potential for a lawsuit if this is not handled properly?	Yes (3)	Maybe (2)	No (1)
How confident do you feel about the actions you need to/should take in this situation?	Very confident (1)	Somewhat confident (2)	Not confident (3)
Have you followed the policy and procedures set by the board and have appropriate documentation for the issue?	Yes (1)	Maybe (2)	No (3)
Does the issue relate to any of these topics? • Litigation • EEOC complaint • Human rights violation (if applicable in state) • Union collective bargaining • Union issues beyond the contract • Harassment/ discrimination claim • Workers' compensation claim	Yes (10)	Maybe (10)	No (1)

TOTAL: _____

SCORE

5–7:   You do not have to call an attorney and seem equipped to handle this issue yourself. But if you have any doubts, you should call.

8–12:   You probably should call an attorney. You have some experience but you do not feel confident in handling this on your own. To play it safe, call the attorney. If you feel like throwing caution to the wind (we don't recommend that), handle it on your own.

13–22:   Call the attorney. Did you call yet? Go call.

||||||||||||||||||||||||||||||||||||||||||||||||||||||||||||||||||||||||||||||||||||||||||||||||||||||||||||||||||

DISCIPLINE PHILOSOPHY

In order to ensure all employees are being treated equitably across your organization, you need to ensure anyone supervising employees is on the same page in terms of how discipline is handled. The discipline philosophy should be created and shared across all supervisors.

PHILOSOPHICAL
- What is the library's mission?
- What is the library's vision?
- What are the library's values?
- How should the mission, vision, and values play into discipline in the organization?
- How do we want to hold staff accountable?
- How do we ensure we are treating employees equitably across departments in terms of holding staff accountable?
- How do we want to handle escalation of an issue?
- Do we hold different positions, departments, or other groups of staff accountable in different ways?
- How do we ensure that disciplinary action across the library does not disproportionately impact traditionally marginalized staff?
- How do we ensure we are removing bias from our compensation decisions?

PRACTICAL
- How do we convey expectations to staff for work performed?
- What are non-negotiables in terms of when discipline needs to occur?
- What are items in the employee handbook/personnel policies that, if broken, would necessitate disciplinary action?

LIBRARY DISCIPLINE PHILOSOPHY

Based on the answers to the questions above, write 1–2 sentences on what you see as your library's discipline philosophy. Depending on how in sync everyone is, you may also want to provide examples of some of the non-negotiables that will always require disciplinary action.

SAMPLE 11.2

||||||||||||||||||||||||||||||||||||||||||||||||||||||||||||||||||||||||||||||||||||||||||||||||||||||||||||

DISCIPLINE AND TERMINATION CHECKLIST

STEP 1—Verbal Warning
- ☐ Verbal warning
- ☐ Script for meeting
- ☐ Follow-up email

STEP 2—Written Warning
- ☐ Write up warning
- ☐ File warning in employee file
- ☐ Provide copy to employee
- ☐ Write up what happened at the meeting to deliver written warning

STEP 3—Second written warning or suspension or professional improvement plan
- ☐ Write up warning/suspension letter/professional improvement plan
- ☐ Provide employee with signed copy
- ☐ File signed copy in employee file
- ☐ Write up what happened at the meeting

STEP 4—Termination
- ☐ Write a script for the termination meeting
- ☐ Prepare termination letter
- ☐ Prepare paperwork (COBRA, unemployment pamphlet, vacation payout)
- ☐ Provide employee with signed term letter
- ☐ File signed copy of term letter in employee file
- ☐ File with unemployment office

SAMPLE 11.3

||||||||||||||||||||||||||||||||||||||||||||||||||||||||||||||||||||||||||||||||||||||||||||||||||||||||||||||||||||||

WRITTEN WARNING WORKSHEET

1. What is the reason for the discipline?
   - Work product
   - Procedural
   - Policy violation
   - Behavioral

2. What documentation are you keeping on this issue? Include date, time, info on issue.

3. Discrimination/unconscious bias check:
   - Is the employee in a protected class?
   - If yes, are you treating this employee differently than an employee not in a protected class with similar issues?
   - If a star employee had the same issue, how would you handle the situation?
   - Are you holding this employee to the same set of guidelines and standards as any other employee?
   - Are you being consistent in holding all employees accountable to the same set of expectations?

SAMPLE 12.1

||||||||||||||||||||||||||||||||||||||||||||||||||||||||||||||||||||||||||||||||||||||||||||||||||||||||||||||||

MANAGER OFFBOARDING CHECKLIST

Employee Name: _____   **Department:** _____

Position: _____

Last Day Worked: _____   **Date of Final Paycheck:** _____

BEFORE DEPARTURE

☐ Request resignation letter from employee/manager.

☐ Provide employee with exit questionnaire.

☐ Schedule exit interview.

☐ Conduct exit interview.

☐ Ask for personal email and if last paycheck will be picked up or mailed.

☐ Advise on final payroll and any vacation payout.

☐ Advise employee to call about pension (if applicable).

☐ Advise employee to call about 457b.

☐ Prepare and provide employee with COBRA letter (medical and/or dental).

☐ Check if director needs access to terminated employee's email or files.

☐ Determine if there are any digital/paper files that need to be kept for records retention.

☐ Check if employee is registered for future dated seminars or conferences and try to cancel.

☐ Advise on flex spending/HSA/HRA.

☐ Ask for list of all passwords.

☐ If retiring, ask about celebration.

LAST DAY

- ☐ Collect employee handbook.
- ☐ Collect access card/keys/fob.
- ☐ Collect equipment.
- ☐ Ensure that away message with who to contact is on email and voicemail.
- ☐ Shut off computer access, change passwords.
- ☐ Ensure work area is cleared of all personal belongings.

AFTER DEPARTURE

- ☐ Change passwords.
- ☐ Move medical file from active to terminated.
- ☐ Remove from flex spending/HSA/HRA.
- ☐ Complete any termination paperwork for pension and send in.
- ☐ Terminate and process personnel jacket on personnel file.
- ☐ Pull I-9 form from active binder; enter and file form in the terminated I-9 binder.
- ☐ Delete from medical insurance.
- ☐ Delete from life insurance.
- ☐ Remove from life insurance coverage.
- ☐ Process final paycheck and cease direct deposits (if applicable).
- ☐ Stop all vacation, sick, etc. accruals.
- ☐ Enter unemployment info.
- ☐ Transfer benefit file to terminated section of files.
- ☐ Remove from photo directory.
- ☐ Remove from telephone directory.
- ☐ Enter into position turnover report.
- ☐ Move digital/paper files that need to be kept for records retention to secure location.
- ☐ Send IT ticket to archive and remove accounts:
    - ☐ If director responded "Y" to needing access to staff email or files, include in the email: "Please reset passwords for Google and active directory accounts and give to department manager."
    - ☐ If director responded "N," include in the email: "Please archive email and remove Google account."

- ☐ Transfer ownership of drive files to department manager.
- ☐ Deactivate access card.
- ☐ Notify Circulation manager (of termination to delete staff library card/change to patron-only status).

- ☐ Delete from regional library system database.
- ☐ Remove from phone list, emergency closing list, CPR/AED list, etc.
- ☐ Remove name from mailbox.
- ☐ Go through work area and organize/clean files and desk.

INDEX

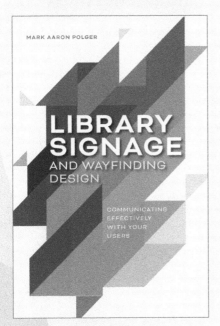